APP for Reading and Writing

Year 3

Christine Moorcroft

Contents

Introduction

APP for Reading and Writing has been developed to help you accurately assess your pupils' progress and attainment in reading and writing skills, using texts and questions designed to elicit evidence for specific assessment points. This Year 3 file contains six tasks, covering the Assessment Foci for National Curriculum Levels 2 and 3.

How to use this book

The tasks in this book are designed to support the periodic assessment that is a key part of the 'Assessing Pupils' Progress' (APP) evidence gathering. The tasks help you to gather evidence to support your own professional understanding of each child's level of achievement. The tasks should help you form a good understanding of the National Curriculum level at which children are working. They have been written to work in conjunction with, and should be used alongside, the QCDA and National Strategy APP Assessment Guidance charts and the Standards files. Copies of the Assessment Guidance charts are included on pages 5 and 6.

Gathering assessment evidence to address Assessment Foci

The Assessment Guidance charts on pages 5 and 6 outline the Assessment Foci for Reading and Writing, all of which are covered by the tasks in this book. The chart on the top of page 4 gives an overview of this coverage. Where a child is not demonstrating the reading and / or writing evidence expected at Level 2 in these tasks, you may want to find an equivalent task from the Year 1 or Year 2 books to collect evidence across Levels 1 and 2. The tasks cover the same Assessment Foci although the genre of the stimulus pieces may differ.

Using the tasks in the classroom

There are six tasks in this book, which can be integrated into your school's literacy planning. The tasks are based on stimulus pieces from a variety of fiction and non-fiction text types. Each of the tasks allows you to collect evidence for both reading and writing. The tasks may also provide evidence about pupils' attainment and progress in speaking and listening. We recommend that children carry out the reading activity first, so that they are familiar with the stimulus piece before completing the writing activity. Each task is designed to take approximately 30 minutes to complete. The tasks will support your evidence gathering, but will not be the sole basis for your judgements about pupils' achievement.

Teacher Sheets

Each task has a Teacher Sheet offering an overview of the task, the key concepts it targets and the related Renewed Framework unit and objectives it covers.

Reading tasks

You can choose between working with a small group for guided reading, or asking children to read and answer the questions independently. The guided reading questions are supplied on the Teacher Sheet for each task. You might like to use these to collect evidence through open discussion, in which case you can use the Reading Responses Levelling Guidance sheet to capture notes about individual oral responses. If you would rather ask children to work independently, the questions and space to answer them are provided on the photocopiable sheets for each task. The bold questions on the Teacher Sheet are those that are included on the photocopiable Reading Response Sheets.

For both guided and independent reading, the questions focus on two or three AFs, and the assessment guidance sheet gives you examples of the kind of responses children may give, and the level this would indicate.

Writing tasks

For writing, children complete a series of short-answer questions and a longer writing activity. Real examples of children's work are provided, along with notes to help you assess children's work for all the Assessment Foci. It should be noted that responses can vary within a level depending on the type of writing pupils are asked to do (e.g. some may not do as well with narrative as they do with a report). Therefore, attainment and progress for any pupil should not be expected to be totally linear.

Making assessment judgements

No single task can determine that a child is low, secure or high Level 2 or Level 3. However, observing a child working on several tasks over a period of time will provide evidence of their functioning at a particular level for reading and writing and should also give an indication of their security within that level. You will need to combine the evidence that these tasks give you with your day-to-day knowledge of a child's performance to decide how consistently the evidence fits the criteria in the Assessment Focus in order to determine whether the child's performance at that level is 'low', 'secure' or 'high'. You should also gather evidence for reading and writing from other subject areas.

A child may prove to be at different levels for different Assessment Foci, and be at a different level for reading than for writing. When you highlight the areas at which they are working on the assessment grids, you may see a 'spiky profile'; you can use this to inform your future planning to fill in any gaps in children's knowledge or skills by referring to the learning objectives that underpin that particular Assessment Focus.

Consistency and moderation

The example answers provided in this book are designed to help you gauge the level at which the children in your class are performing. However, these examples are provided as a guide only and professional judgement must be used when reviewing the evidence and making consistent judgements about children's attainment. The examples cannot cover all the different ways in which different children may respond. When you are reviewing the evidence from these tasks, along with other evidence, to make a level judgement, it is good practice to confer with a colleague who knows the children's performance in literacy to corroborate your judgement.

What to do next

At the end of each task, 'next steps' guidance is given about what teachers might do next in terms of planning for teaching and learning for the relevant AFs, referenced to the appropriate learning objectives. This guidance also points to other assessments within the book that cover those AFs.

Assessment Foci covered by the Year 3 tasks

● = Main AFs   O = Other AFs

READING	AF1	AF2	AF3	AF4	AF5	AF6	AF7	
Task 1: Fun at the Fair	O	O	●		●	O		
Task 2: At the End of School Assembly	O	O		●	●			
Task 3: Too Much Searching	O	●	O	●		O	●	
Task 4: How to Recycle Paper		●	●	●	O	O		
Task 5: Flood!	O	●		●	O			
Task 6: Frogs and Toads		●		●		●		

WRITING	AF1	AF2	AF3	AF4	AF5	AF6	AF7	AF8
Task 1: Fun at the Fair	●					●	●	
Task 2: At the End of School Assembly	O	●	●				●	O
Task 3: Too Much Searching	O	●	●	●				O
Task 4: How to Recycle Paper		●	●			●		O
Task 5: Flood!	O		●		●		●	
Task 6: Frogs and Toads	●	●	●			O	O	

Renewed Framework for Literacy Reading and Writing Objectives covered by the Year 3 tasks

7. **Understanding and interpreting texts**
   - 7.1 Infer characters' feelings in fiction and consequences in logical explanations
   - 7.2 Identify and make notes of the main points of the section(s) of text
   - 7.3 Identify how different texts are organised, including reference texts, magazines and leaflets, on paper and on screen
   - 7.4 Use syntax, context and word structure to build their store of vocabulary as they read for meaning
   - 7.5 Explore how different texts appeal to readers using varied sentence structures and descriptive language

8. **Engaging with and responding to texts**
   - 8.2 Empathise with characters and debate moral dilemmas portrayed in texts
   - 8.3 Identify features that writers use to provoke readers' reactions

9. **Creating and shaping texts**
   - 9.1 Make decisions about form and purpose, identify success criteria and use them to evaluate their writing
   - 9.2 Use beginning, middle and end to write narratives in which events are sequenced logically and conflicts resolved.
   - 9.3 Write non-narrative texts using structures of different text-types
   - 9.4 Select and use a range of technical and descriptive vocabulary

10. **Text structure and organisation**
    - 10.1 Signal sequence, place and time to give coherence
    - 10.2 Group related material into paragraphs

11. **Sentence structure and punctuation**
    - 11.1 Show relationships of time, reason and cause through subordination and connectives
    - 11.2 Compose sentences using adjectives, verbs and nouns for precision, clarity and impact
    - 11.3 Clarify meaning through the use of exclamation marks and speech marks

Task	Renewed Framework objectives covered
Task 1: Fun at the Fair	7.1, 7.2, 8.2, 9.4, 11.2, 11.3
Task 2: At the End of School Assembly	7.2, 7.4, 7.5, 8.3, 9.1, 9.3
Task 3: Too Much Searching	7.1, 7.4, 8.3, 9.4, 10.2
Task 4: How to Recycle Paper	7.2, 7.3, 9.3, 9.4, 10.2, 11.2
Task 5: Flood!	7.1, 9.1, 9.2, 9.4, 10.1, 11.1
Task 6: Frogs and Toads	7.3, 9.1, 9.3, 9.4, 11.2

QCDA Reading Assessment Guidelines: Levels 2 and 3

	AF1 – use a range of strategies, including accurate decoding of text, to read for meaning	AF2 – understand, describe, select or retrieve information, events or ideas from texts and use quotation and reference to text	AF3 – deduce, infer or interpret information, events or ideas from texts	AF4 – identify and comment on the structure and organisation of texts, including grammatical and presentational features at text level	AF5 – explain and comment on writers' use of language, including grammatical and literary features at word and sentence level	AF6 – identify and comment on writers' purposes and viewpoints, and the overall effect of the text on the reader	AF7 – relate texts to their social, cultural and historical traditions
L3	**In most reading** • range of strategies used mostly effectively to read with fluency, understanding and expression	**In most reading** • simple, most obvious points identified though there may also be some misunderstanding, e.g. about information from different places in the text • some comments include quotations from or references to text, but not always relevant, e.g. often retelling or paraphrasing sections of the text rather than using it to support comment	**In most reading** • straightforward inference based on a single point of reference in the text, e.g. 'he was upset because it says "he was crying"' • responses to text show meaning established at a literal level e.g. '"walking good" means "walking carefully"' or based on personal speculation e.g. a response based on what they personally would be feeling rather than feelings of character in the text	**In most reading** • a few basic features of organisation at text level identified, with little or no linked comment, e.g. 'it tells about all the different things you can do at the zoo'	**In most reading** • a few basic features of writer's use of language identified, but with little or no comment, e.g. 'there are lots of adjectives' or 'he uses speech marks to show there are lots of people there'	**In most reading** • comments identify main purpose, e.g. 'the writer doesn't like violence' • express personal response but with little awareness of writer's viewpoint or effect on reader, e.g. 'she was just horrible like my nan is sometimes'	**In most reading** • some simple connections between texts identified, e.g. similarities in plot, topic, or books by same author, about same characters • recognition of some features of the context of texts, e.g. historical setting, social or cultural background
L2	**In some reading** • range of key words read on sight • unfamiliar words decoded using appropriate strategies, e.g. blending sounds • some fluency and expression, e.g. taking account of speech marks, punctuation	**In some reading** • some specific, straightforward information recalled, e.g. names of characters, main ingredients • generally clear idea of where to look for information, e.g. about characters, topics	**In some reading** • simple, plausible inference about events and information, using evidence from text, e.g. how a character is feeling, what makes a plant grow • comments based on textual cues, sometimes misunderstood	**In some reading** • some awareness of use of features of organisation, e.g. beginning and ending of story, types of punctuation	**In some reading** • some effective language choices noted, e.g. '"slimy" is a good word there' • some familiar patterns of language identified, e.g. once upon a time; first, next, last	**In some reading** • some awareness that writers have viewpoints and purposes, e.g. 'it tells you how to do something', 'she thinks it's not fair' • simple statements about likes and dislikes in reading, sometimes with reasons	**In some reading** • general features of a few text types identified, e.g. information books, stories, print media • some awareness that books are set in different times and places
BL							
IE							

Overall assessment (tick one box only)   Low 2 [ ]   Secure 2 [ ]   High 2 [ ]   Low 3 [ ]   Secure 3 [ ]   High 3 [ ]   BL = 'Below Level'   IE = 'Insufficient Evidence'

QCDA Writing Assessment Guidelines: Levels 2 and 3

	AF5 – vary sentences for clarity, purpose and effect	AF6 – write with technical accuracy of syntax and punctuation in phrases, clauses and sentences	AF3 – organise and present whole texts effectively, sequencing and structuring information, ideas and events	AF4 – construct paragraphs and use cohesion within and between paragraphs	AF1 – write imaginative, interesting and thoughtful texts	AF2 – produce texts which are appropriate to task, reader and purpose	AF7 – select appropriate and effective vocabulary	AF8 – use correct spelling	Handwriting and presentation
L3	**In most writing** • reliance mainly on simply structured sentences, variation with support, e.g. some complex sentences • and, but, so are the most common connectives, subordination occasionally • some limited variation in use of tense and verb forms, not always secure	**In most writing** • straightforward sentences usually demarcated accurately with full stops, capital letters, question and exclamation marks • some, limited, use of speech punctuation • comma splicing evident, particularly in narrative	**In most writing** • some attempt to organise ideas with related points placed next to each other • openings and closings usually signalled • some attempt to sequence ideas or material logically	**In most writing** • some internal structure within sections of text e.g. one-sentence paragraphs or ideas loosely organised • within paragraphs/sections, some links between sentences, e.g. use of pronouns or of adverbials • movement between paragraphs/sections sometimes abrupt or disjointed	**In most writing** • some appropriate ideas and content included • some attempt to elaborate on basic information or events, e.g. nouns expanded by simple adjectives • attempt to adopt viewpoint, though often not maintained or inconsistent, e.g. attitude expressed, but with little elaboration	**In most writing** • purpose established at a general level • main features of selected form sometimes signalled to the reader • some attempts at appropriate style, with attention to reader	**In most writing** • simple, generally appropriate vocabulary used, limited in range • some words selected for effect or occasion	**In most writing** • correct spelling of – some common grammatical function words – common content/lexical words with more than one morpheme, including compound words • likely errors – some inflected endings, e.g. past tense, comparatives, adverbs – some phonetically plausible attempts at content/lexical words	**In most writing** • legible style, shows accurate and consistent letter formation, sometimes joined
L2	**In some forms of writing** • some variation in sentence openings, e.g. not always starting with name or pronoun • mainly simple sentences with and used to connect clauses • past and present tense generally consistent	**In some forms of writing** • clause structure mostly grammatically correct • sentence demarcation with capital letters and full stops usually accurate • some accurate use of question and exclamation marks, and commas in lists	**In some forms of writing** • some basic sequencing of ideas or material, e.g. time-related words or phrases, line breaks, headings, numbers • openings and/or closings sometimes signalled	**In some forms of writing** • ideas in sections grouped by content, some linking by simple pronouns	**In some forms of writing** • mostly relevant ideas and content, sometimes repetitive or sparse • some apt word choices create interest • brief comments, questions about events or actions suggest viewpoint	**In some forms of writing** • some basic purpose established, e.g. main features of story, report • some appropriate features of the given form used • some attempts to adopt appropriate style	**In some forms of writing** • simple, often speech-like vocabulary conveys relevant meanings • some adventurous word choices, e.g. opportune use of new vocabulary	**In some forms of writing** • usually correct spelling of – high frequency grammatical function words – common single-morpheme content/lexical words • likely errors – inflected endings, e.g. past tense, plurals, adverbs – phonetic attempts at vowel digraphs	**In some forms of writing** • letters generally correctly shaped but inconsistencies in orientation, size and use of upper/lower case letters • clear letter formation, with ascenders and descenders distinguished, generally upper and lower case letters not mixed within words
BL									
IE									

Overall assessment (tick one box only)   Low 2 ☐   Secure 2 ☐   High 2 ☐   Low 3 ☐   Secure 3 ☐   High 3 ☐   BL = 'Below Level'   IE = 'Insufficient Evidence'

Task 1 Fun at the Fair

Aims of this task

This task is designed to help you to make judgements about children's attainment in Reading **AF3** and **AF5** (with opportunities to assess **AF1**, **AF2** and **AF6** as well) and Writing **AF1**, **AF6** and **AF7**. The children read and respond to a story about a family's day out at a funfair, which depicts a brother and sister's differing feelings and a trick that one plays on the other. The children write dialogue for their own version of the trick.

Related Renewed Framework unit

Narrative Unit 1: Stories with familiar settings

Renewed Framework objectives

7.1, 7.2, 8.2, 9.4, 11.2, 11.3

Key concepts
Reading
- infer characters' feelings and interpret events from the text (AF3)
- explain and comment on writer's use of descriptive language (AF5)
- identify and comment on the author's viewpoint (AF6)

Writing
- write imaginative and appropriate dialogue (AF1)
- compose well-structured and appropriately punctuated sentences (AF6)
- select appropriate words and phrases to describe a funfair (AF7)

Questions for guided reading

Starting off

Ask what the children know about funfairs. What can they do there? What feelings do funfairs bring to mind? Ask them to read the story (AF1) and think about the feelings of the characters.

Read and respond

To check that the children have understood the passage, ask them to contribute to a group discussion, using the following prompts:

- Who went on the waltzer with Megan? (AF2)
- **What did David have to do to win the trick lollipop? (AF2)**
- How did David trick Megan? (AF2)
- **Why did the family split up to do different things at the fair? Why didn't they all go on the waltzer? (AF3)**
- **Why do you think the author had Megan call David a 'scaredy-cat'? (AF5)**
- **How did David feel about being called a 'scaredy-cat'? (AF3)**

Going deeper

- **Explain why the author chose to call the stall 'Trick or Sweet'. (AF5)**
- **How did Megan feel when she bit the lollipop? How do you know? (AF3)**
- **How did David and Megan's feelings change through the story? (AF3)**

Reflect

Discuss what the children think is the message of the story. **What does the story tell us about funfairs?** What does it say about playing tricks and having tricks played on you? (AF6)

Task 1 Fun at the Fair by Jenny Alexander

Mum, Dad, Megan and David were at the fair.

"Come on!" shouted Megan excitedly as she looked at all the thrilling rides. "Let's go on the waltzer!"

David watched as the seats rose and fell like boats on a stormy sea and the people screamed. He clutched Mum's hand and shook his head.

"Scaredy-cat!" teased Megan.

So Dad went on the waltzer with Megan. Mum and David found a stall with a game called 'Trick or Sweet?'

You had to turn over a card and if it was red, you won some real sweets, but if it was black, you won some trick sweets. David won a trick lollipop. It looked just like a real one, but it was made of rubber.

They went back to the waltzer just as Megan and Dad were getting off.

"That was wicked!" Megan said. "It's a shame you're such a scaredy-cat, David. You're missing all the fun!"

David shrugged. "I got you a lollipop," he said. He held it out to her. Megan took it and tried to take a bite. Then she looked at it more closely and began to grin. Soon everyone was laughing.

"There are lots of different ways of having fun at the funfair!" said Mum.

Task 1 Fun at the Fair

1. What did David have to do to win the trick lollipop?

2. Why did the family split up to do different things at the fair? Why didn't they all go on the waltzer?

3. Why do you think the author had Megan call David a 'scaredy-cat'?

4. Write how David felt about being called a 'scaredy-cat' in the thought bubble.

Task 1 Fun at the Fair

5. Explain why the author chose to call the stall 'Trick or Sweet'.

6. How did Megan feel when she bit the lollipop? How do you know?

7. How did David and Megan's feelings change through the story?

8. What does the story tell us about funfairs?

Task 1 Fun at the Fair

Main Assessment Focus: AF3 (deduce, infer or interpret information, events or ideas from texts)

Question	Exemplified responses	Grid reference	Notes
How did David feel about being called a 'scaredy-cat'?	Simple, plausible inference: 'He didn't mind.'	Level 2 / bullet 1	
	Textual cues, sometimes misunderstood: 'He thought it was good and he gave Megan a lollipop.'	Level 2 / bullet 2	
	Inference from a single point of reference: 'It didn't bother him. It says he shrugged.'	Level 3 / bullet 1	
	Meaning based on own response: 'He was hurt / sad / angry / upset.'	Level 3 / bullet 2	
How did Megan feel when she bit the lollipop? How do you know?	Simple, plausible inference: excited / pleased.	Level 2 / bullet 1	
	Textual cues, sometimes misunderstood: 'She didn't like black lollipops.'	Level 2 / bullet 2	
	Inference from a single point of reference: 'She thought it was funny. It says she grinned.'	Level 3 / bullet 1	
	Meaning established on the basis of own response: 'She was angry.'	Level 3 / bullet 2	
How did David and Megan's feelings change through the story?	Comments on feelings at start: excited. Doesn't track changes of feelings.	Level 2 / bullet 1	
	Inference from a single point of reference: 'David clutched Mum's hand. He was scared of the waltzer.' 'Everyone was happy at the end. It says everyone laughed.'	Level 3 / bullet 1	

Main Assessment Focus: AF5 (explain and comment on writers' use of language, including grammatical and literary features at word and sentence level)

Question	Exemplified responses	Grid reference	Notes
Why do you think the author had Megan call David a 'scaredy-cat'?	Refers back to text, but no comment on appropriateness of language: 'David was scared of the waltzer.'	Level 2 / bullet 1	
	Comments on appropriate choice: 'It's a good word because Megan is teasing David about being scared.'	Level 3 / bullet 1	
Explain why the author chose to call the stall 'Trick or Sweet'.	Literal response: 'You might win a sweet or a trick.'	Level 2 / bullet 2	
	Says it sounds like Halloween trick or treat; might notice rhyme – 'trick or treat'.	Level 3 / bullet 1	

Other Assessment Focus: AF2 (understand, describe, select or retrieve information, events or ideas from texts and use quotation and reference to text)

Question	Exemplified responses	Grid reference	Notes
What did David have to do to win the trick lollipop?	Straightforward information recalled: 'He played "Trick or Sweet".'	Level 2 / bullet 1	
	More precise: 'He had to turn over a card with black on the back.'	Level 3 / bullet 1	

Other Assessment Focus: AF6 (identify and comment on writers' purposes and viewpoints, and the overall effect of the text on the reader)

Question	Exemplified responses	Grid reference	Notes
What does the story tell us about funfairs?	Some awareness of purpose: 'You can have fun at the funfair.'	Level 2 / bullet 1	
	Identifies the main purpose: 'You might like fast rides or quieter things.'	Level 3 / bullet 1	

Exemplified responses matched to levels of attainment are provided as a guide. As always, professional judgement must be used when assessing pupils' learning progression and a range of evidence should be gathered for each AF.

Task 1 Fun at the Fair

1. Write some words and phrases to describe what it is like at a funfair.

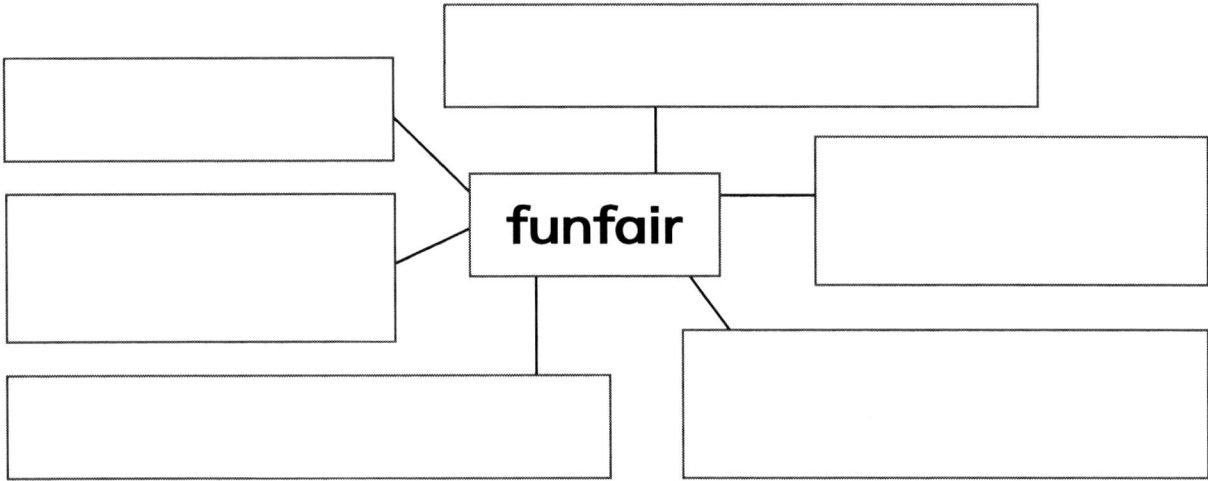

2. Make up a new activity and a different trick for the 'Trick or Sweet?' stall in the story.

   Write in sentences about what you have to do at the stall and what the different 'trick' is.

3. Now, imagine that you won the new trick.

   • How would you play the trick on another child?

   • What might you say to the other child and what might they answer?

   Write the conversation on the back of this sheet or on a separate piece of paper.

Task 1 Fun at the Fair

A pupil response within the range for Level 2 might be:

Question 1 (AF7)

- Most but possibly not all spaces filled; appropriate single-word descriptions (e.g. noisy, exciting) and may include some taken from story (e.g. fun, wicked) and some nouns (e.g. rides, waltzer, prizes); some adventurous word choices (e.g. blaring, thrilling).

Question 2 (AF6)

- At least two simple sentences to describe new stall activity and new trick. Sentences begin with a capital letter and end with a full stop, and initial capitals for names, if used. Words written in an order that makes sense. Some attempt to use past tense, but not consistent. E.g. 'It was a fishing game with numbers on the fish. An even number wins some sweets and an odd number won a joke spider.'

Question 3 (AF1, AF6, AF7)

AF1

Subject matter and content are relevant.

Includes the two characters, though neither is the writer as indicated in the writing task instructions.

Includes new game idea (i.e. darts game), but is not explicit about what new trick sweet is.

Imaginative use of 'got you' at the end to round off idea of trick.

AF6

Clause structures grammatically correct.

Sentence demarcation (capital letters and full stops) usually accurate, though full stop needed after 'now' [know] and capital letter after 'urr!'.

Use of exclamation mark after 'urr'.

AF7

Vocabulary is mostly straightforward and speech-like; conveys relevant meanings. Key words 'trick' and 'sweet' (including 'treat' [treet]) repeated.

Some vocabulary choices suggest deliberate attempt for effect, e.g. 'urr', 'horrible' [horibel], 'got you'.

> Tom won a trick sweet for the darts game. He said to his friend Adam I have a treat for you Gess wich hand x. I don't now Tom gave Adam the trick sweet and wached him eat it. Adam said urr! thats horibel. Tom laughed there he said got you.

Task 1 Fun at the Fair

A pupil response within the range for Level 3 might be:

Question 1 (AF7)

- All spaces filled (and possibly others) with appropriate words and some phrases evoking a funfair atmosphere (e.g. flashing lights, cheerful music, hot-dog smells, screams of delight).

Question 2 (AF6)

- Use of more connectives such as 'but' and 'if'; past tense used mainly consistently; some use of commas to separate clauses. E.g. 'It was a fishing game and you had to catch a fish. If the fish had an even number on it, you won some sweets but if the number was odd, you won a joke spider.'

Question 3 (AF1, AF6, AF7)

AF1

The writing includes appropriate ideas and content, with opening and closing based closely on the model text. Imaginative ending ('that will teach you'). Includes the two characters, though neither is the writer as task indicated.

Includes details of new trick (hook a frog) and new sweet (curry-flavoured chocolate).

Cause and effect indicated by use (overuse) of 'so'.

Some elaboration: nouns expanded by adjectives (e.g. 'plastic', 'whizzing', 'curry flavour').

AF6

Straightforward sentences are mainly demarcated with full stops, capital letters, and use of commas in list (e.g. 'with their mums, Lucy's dad, Jess's brother Sam').

Also attempts to use other punctuation, e.g. dash and exclamation marks.

Mostly accurate use of speech marks.

AF7

Appropriate use of vocabulary relevant to content.

Evidence of words chosen carefully to engage the reader and create effect, e.g. 'whizzing', 'curry flavour', 'greedily', 'popped', 'yuck'.

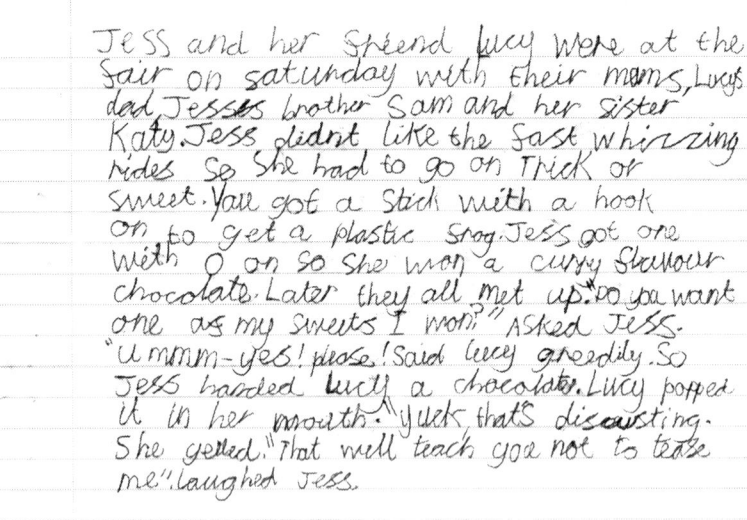

Task 1 Fun at the Fair

Reading

Next steps for developing AF3

Children will benefit from further practice in answering inferential questions and using reference to the text to support answers. Useful questions you could ask when reading a piece of text together might be:

- Why do you think [David] didn't ...?
- Which words in the story make you think that?
- Did [Megan] and [David] feel the same about ...? Which words tell you that?
- How would you feel if...? Did [David] feel like that? Which words tell you that?

This activity should be part of a range of evidence gathered for AF3. Evidence for AF3 can be gathered from various sources, such as:

- observations during guided and shared reading;
- responding to pictures, film, broadcasts etc;
- creating character profiles or completing thought bubbles;
- whenever children need to read between the lines in a text in another subject area: e.g. history, RE or PSHE.

Task 3 on pages 26 to 36 and Task 4 on pages 37 to 46 provide other opportunities to gather evidence for AF3.

Next steps for developing AF5

Children will benefit from further practice in answering questions about language and grammatical features and identifying these in texts. Questions like those below could be asked when reading a piece of text together:

- Which words help you to picture...?
- How does the writer emphasise...?
- What do you notice about the sounds of these words...?

This activity should be part of a range of evidence gathered for AF5. Evidence for AF5 can be gathered from many different sources, such as:

- observations during discussions of poetry;
- responding to performance poems, rhymes and jingles;
- creating character profiles or thought bubbles;
- whenever there are opportunities to think about the effects of words.

Task 2 on pages 17 to 25, Task 4 on pages 37 to 46 and Task 5 on pages 47 to 55 provide other opportunities to gather evidence for AF5.

Writing

Next steps for developing AF1

You could develop the children's skills in writing imaginative and thoughtful stories through exchanging their stories with a partner and giving them points to notice and ideas for questions and discussion:

- What did you like best about the characters? About what happened?
- Would you change anything? What, and how?
- What had been happening before the story began?
- Is there anything that confuses you?
- Would the character really say that?

Task 1 Fun at the Fair

Writing (continued)

Next steps for developing AF1 (continued)

This should be part of a range of writing activities from which evidence is gathered for AF1. Evidence for AF1 can also be gathered from:

- writing playscripts and poetry;
- writing non-fiction texts including reports, information texts, letters, instructions.

Task 2 on pages 17 to 25, Task 3 on pages 26 to 36, Task 5 on pages 47 to 55 and Task 6 on pages 56 to 64 provide other opportunities to gather evidence for AF1.

Next steps for developing AF6

You could develop the children's understanding of syntax, punctuation and sentence structure through the following activities, discussion and questioning:

- reading a short, unpunctuated text on screen using IWB software, deciding where each sentence should begin and end and adding the punctuation;
- reading one another's writing and looking for other missing punctuation: exclamation marks, question marks, commas. Talk about how these help the reader to make sense of the writing;
- removing commas from sentences and suggesting different meanings, which are not clear without commas;
- telling jokes that involve questions and then writing them down.

This should be part of a range of writing activities from which evidence is gathered for AF6. Evidence for AF6 can also be gathered from:

- other narrative writing where punctuation is important for meaning;
- non-fiction writing that includes phrases and clauses linked by time or logical connectives, and finding alternative connectives to avoid repetition;
- transcribing dialogue, using speech marks to make clear what is said by whom.

Task 4 on pages 37 to 46 and Task 6 on pages 56 to 64 provide other opportunities to gather evidence for AF6.

Next steps for developing AF7

You could develop the children's vocabulary and their appreciation of the effects of words through activities and discussions such as:

- picking out effective words from the children's writing and talking about the impression they give the reader: e.g. urr!, got you, whizzing, greedily, popped it in her mouth, yuck, yelled.
- asking if the children can think of better words than one or two of those they used: e.g. laughed / chuckled, yelled / spluttered.
- creating lists of useful connectives, grouped for meaning and purpose, so that the children can select the most effective and avoid repetition: (so) That meant, as a result, because of that; (then) next, later, after that, a few hours later, a few minutes later, after while, straightaway, immediately, right away, eventually.

This should be part of a range of writing activities from which evidence is gathered for AF7. Evidence for AF7 can also be gathered from:

- word lists connected with topics the children have studied in other subjects, including useful connectives used in their recounts or reports;
- previous work on powerful or expressive verbs or adjectives;
- brainstorming words connected with a topic or idea;
- using a thesaurus.

Task 2 on pages 17 to 25, Task 5 on pages 47 to 55 and Task 6 on pages 56 to 64 provide other opportunities to gather evidence for AF7.

Task 2 At the End of School Assembly

Aims of this task

This task is designed to help you to make judgements about children's attainment in Reading **AF4** and **AF5** (with opportunities to assess AF1 and AF2 as well) and Writing **AF2, AF3** and **AF7** (with opportunities to assess AF1 and AF8 as well). The children read and respond to a non-rhyming word-play poem. They think of some imaginative and powerful verbs and then write a verse of their own for the poem.

Key concepts

Reading
- describe features of the poem: e.g. changes in line lengths, no rhyme, lines begin with teacher's name (AF4)
- identify and explain examples of humorous word-play in the poem (AF5)

Writing
- write own verse using the poem as a model (AF2, AF3, AF7)
- select and use effective verbs for moving (AF7)

Related Renewed Framework unit

Poetry Unit 3: Language play

Renewed Framework objectives

7.2, 7.4, 7.5, 8.3, 9.1, 9.3

Questions for guided reading

Starting off

Remind the children of any previous learning about word-play. Ask them to read the poem (AF1). Explain some of the more difficult words; e.g. *steed, ferry, stretcher*. Ask if they know what a *brook* is. Look at the teachers' names and the words for how the classes leave assembly, and imagine each one. The children could also enact the poem.

Read and respond

Answer the following questions as part of a group discussion:
- **Which teacher's class were wheeled out, got herded out, thundered out? (AF2)**
- **Choose your favourite line. What makes it a good word-play? (AF5)**
- **Whose classes *could* have charged out, trotted out, steamed out? (AF5)**
- **How are the lines of the poem alike?** Think about how they begin and end and what is in the middle. **(AF4)**

Going deeper

- **What do you notice about the shape of the poem? How does it sound? (AF4)**
- **What type of non-fiction text is the poem like? (AF4)**
- **Find a word-play in the poem that uses homophones (words that sound the same but have different meanings). (AF5)**

Reflect

Discuss other word-plays that require knowledge of figures of speech: e.g. buzzed off, made tracks, got their skates on. Introduce others and ask the children to come up with teachers' names to match: tripped out (Dance), pushed off (Pram, Buggy), legged it (Spider), beat it (Egg, Whisk), cleared off (Sweep), were frogmarched (Frog), were shepherded out (Sheep, Flock, Lamb), rolled out, bounced out (Ball). (AF5)

Task 2 At the End of School Assembly
by Simon Pitt

At the End of School Assembly

Miss Sparrow's lot flew out,
Mrs Steed's lot galloped out,
Mr Bull's lot got herded out,
Mrs Bumble's lot buzzed off.

Miss Rose's class… rose,
Mr Beetle's class… beetled off,
Miss Storm's class thundered out,
Mrs Frisby's class whirled across the hall.

Mr Train's lot made tracks,
Miss Ferry's lot sailed off,
Mr Roller's lot got their skates on,
Mrs Street's lot got stuck
halfway across.

Mr Idle's class just couldn't be bothered,
Mrs Barrow's class were wheeled out,
Miss Stretcher's class were carried out
And
Mrs Brook's class
Simply
trickled away

Simon Pitt

Task 2 At the End of School Assembly

1. Which teacher's class:

   • were wheeled out? ....

   • got herded out? ....

   • thundered out? ....

2. Choose your favourite line. What makes it a good word-play?

   ....

   ....

   ....

   ....

3. Whose class *could* have charged out? Explain your answer.

   ....

   ....

   ....

4. Whose class *could* have trotted out? Explain your answer.

   ....

   ....

   ....

Task 2 At the End of School Assembly

5. Whose class *could* have steamed out? Explain your answer.

6. How are the lines of the poem alike?

7. What type of non-fiction text is the poem like? Explain your answer.

8. Find a word-play in the poem that uses homophones (words that sound the same but have different meanings). Explain it.

Task 2 At the End of School Assembly

Task 2 At the End of School Assembly

Main Assessment Focus: AF4 (identify and comment on the structure and organisation of texts, including grammatical and presentational features at text level)

Question	Exemplified responses	Grid reference	Notes
How are the lines of the poem alike?	Tends to look at content rather than structure: 'Each line is about how a class goes out of assembly.'	Level 2	
	Notices lines begin with teacher's name, then say how class goes out of assembly. Might notice that lines are sentences but without full stop.	Level 3	
What type of non-fiction text is the poem like? Explain your answer.	Knows what non-fiction means and can give an example of a non-fiction text but might not notice the list format.	Level 2	
	Can select the appropriate text type from the examples given and might be able to describe the shape of a list and relate it to the poem.	Level 3	

Main Assessment Focus: AF5 (explain and comment on writers' use of language, including grammatical and literacy features at word and sentence level)

Question	Exemplified responses	Grid reference	Notes
Choose your favourite line. What makes it a good word-play?	Chooses a line and comments on own response: 'I thought of children in a wheelbarrow', 'I liked the children thundering, stamping their feet'.	Level 2 / bullet 1	
	Chooses a line and makes a link between verb and teacher's name: 'They couldn't be bothered because they were idle like their teacher's name.'	Level 3	
Whose classes could have charged out, trotted out, steamed out?	Plausible choices using names from poem but no real links with names: 'Mrs Barrow's class could charge if the barrow went fast.'	Level 2 / bullet 1	
	Choices linked with word-play. Comments show reasoning: 'Mr Bull's class charged because bulls can charge.'	Level 3	
Find a word-play in the poem that uses homophones (words that sound the same but have different meanings). Explain it.	Might notice repeated words but not appreciate the homophone: rose/rose, beetle/beetled.	Level 2 / bullet 2	
	Shows homophone understood: Explains different meanings of rose.	Level 3	

Other Assessment Focus: AF2 (understand, describe, select or retrieve information, events or ideas from texts and use quotation and reference to text)

Question	Exemplified responses	Grid reference	Notes
Which teachers' classes were wheeled out, got herded out and thundered out?	Words from poem recalled or checked by re-reading.	Level 2 / bullet 1	
	Recalls the details and makes comments about how they remembered: 'You wheel a barrow'; 'Bulls go in herds'; 'You get thunder in a storm'.	Level 3 / bullet 2	

Exemplified responses matched to levels of attainment are provided as a guide. As always, professional judgement must be used when assessing pupils' learning progression and a range of evidence should be gathered for each AF.

Task 2 At the End of School Assembly

1. Write some powerful verbs for moving.

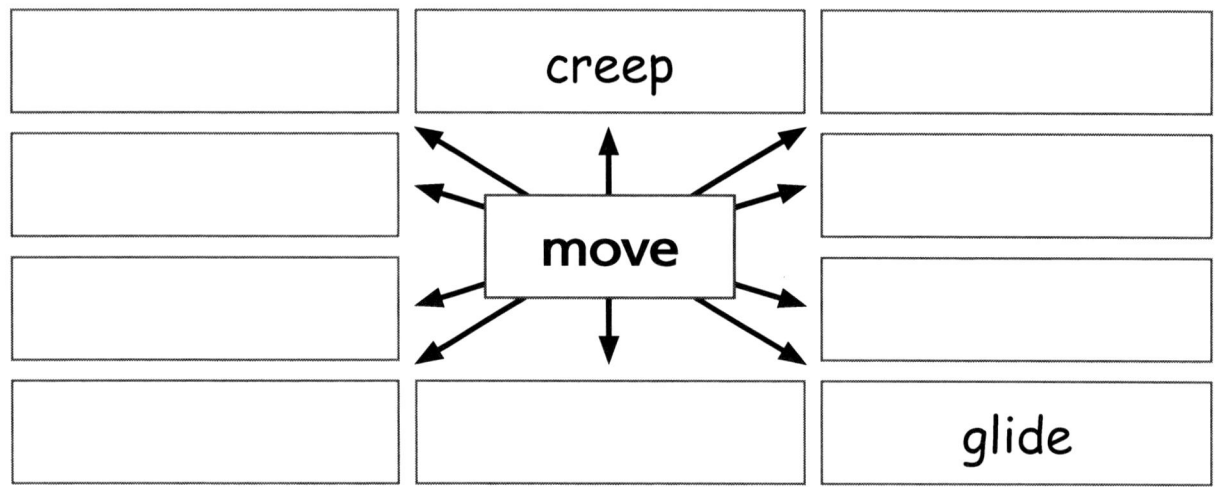

	creep	
	move	
		glide

2. Choose some of your powerful verbs for moving. For each one, write a teacher's name to go with it.

3. Use your ideas from questions 1 and 2 to help you write a new verse for the poem.

Task 2 At the End of School Assembly

A pupil response within the range for Level 2 might be:

Question 1 (AF7)

- All words listed are verbs. A few fairly imaginative verbs (e.g. step, hop); some less so (e.g. run, hurry, jump).

Question 2 (AF7)

- Some names to match the verbs in word-play: Miss Rabbit's class hopped out, Mr Stair's class stepped out.

Question 3 (AF1, AF2, AF3, AF7, AF8)

AF1
Good matches between verbs for moving and teachers' names. Imaginative and interesting.

AF2
Generally follows the format, features and style of model poem well to create own verse.

AF3
Clearly understands the structure of the poem and is able to follow the sentence structure of individual lines and the 4-line verse pattern with appropriate line breaks.

Miss skateboard's class glide out
Miss Burgler's class sneek out
mr Race's lot ran off throgh the door
Mrs Rope's class skipt out

AF7
First line 'lifts' one of the verbs already given on Writing Response Sheet for Question 1 and thus is in present tense instead of past tense, as is verb in line 2, though lines 3 and 4 have appropriate past-tense verbs. 'Ran' in line 3 is not an adventurous word choice, but 'sneak' and 'skipped' and their links with teachers' names display imagination and creativity.

AF8
Most high-frequency words spelled correctly ('the', 'ran', 'off', 'out', 'lot'), and phonetically plausible attempts at content / lexical words (e.g. 'skateboard', 'sneak' and 'burglar'). Errors in more difficult high-frequency words ('through') and inflected endings ('skipt').

Task 2 At the End of School Assembly

A pupil response within the range for Level 3 might be:

Question 1 (AF7)
- All words listed are verbs, some imaginative (e.g. wriggle, bounce); some copied from poem: e.g. gallop, thunder).

Question 2 (AF2)
- Some imaginative word-play: e.g. Miss Worm – wriggled, Mr Snail – slid, Mrs Bat – flitted, Miss Butterfly – fluttered.

Question 3 (AF3)

AF1

Appropriate ideas and content: a poem about classes leaving assembly in a way that reflects their teachers' names, using a range of titles for teachers, as in the model poem: Mrs, Dr, Mr.

Attempts to elaborate by adding a clause: e.g. 'bounced out across the playground'.

AF2

Main features of the model poem used: follows the line rhythm and extends the final line, although the verse has six instead of four lines.

AF3

Sequences ideas as in the model poem.

Closing signalled with the last line with the insertion of 'and' to precede it.

AF7

Appropriate vocabulary, with verbs for movement very well matched to teachers' names. Chooses these well for effect: 'dreamed out', 'slithered out', 'sneaked out'.

AF8

Correct spelling of most words, including words with more than one morpheme: 'slithered', 'sneaked', 'trotted'; also compound words: e.g. 'playground'.

Proofreads and corrects own mistake in inflected ending (hoped / hopped).

> At the end of School
> asembly
>
> Mrs Rabbits class hoped out,
> Mr Beds class dreamed out,
> Dr snails class slithered out,
> Mrs Horses class trotted out,
> Dr Robbers class sneaked out,
> And
> Mrs kangaroos class bounced out
> onto the play ground.

Task 2 At the End of School Assembly

Reading

Next steps for developing AF4

You could develop the children's understanding of the structure and organisation of poems though discussion points and questions such as:

- Are there rhymes in this poem?
- What happens to the lengths of the lines through each verse?
- Where can you find this word / phrase later in the poem?

This activity should be part of a range of evidence gathered for AF4. Evidence for AF4 can also be gathered from a range of other sources, such as:

- observations during guided and shared reading;
- discussion of the structures of different poems (e.g. calligrams, haiku, limericks).

Tasks 3 to 6 on pages 26 to 64 provide other opportunities to gather evidence for AF4.

Next steps for developing AF5

Children will benefit from further practice in answering questions about language and grammatical features and identifying these in texts. When reading together:

- look for verbs that are more interesting than 'go' or 'walk';
- listen to the verbs and see if you can move like that;
- discuss words that have meanings other than the meaning in the poem or story.

This activity should be part of a range of evidence gathered for AF5. Evidence for AF5 can be gathered from a range of sources, such as:

- observations during discussions and performances of poetry;
- whenever there are opportunities to think about the effects of words.

Task 1 on pages 7 to 16 and Tasks 4 and 5 on pages 37 to 55 provide other opportunities to gather evidence for AF5.

Writing

Next steps for developing AF2

Provide further practice for developing poetry writing, for example:

- in shared and guided writing activities, work on simple poems to demonstrate the way poems are formed (structure, etc);
- provide simple pattern structures and other poems to support children's writing;
- encourage children to rehearse their ideas orally.

Tasks 3 and 4 on pages 26 to 46 and Task 6 on pages 56 to 64 provide other opportunities to gather evidence for AF2.

Next steps for developing AF3

Provide further practice for developing structure in poetry writing, for example:

- identify verses, line lengths, syllables, rhyme patterns in poems read;
- use simple structures in shared and guided writing activities as models;
- re-read own and each others' poems to identify points for improvement.

Tasks 3 to 6 on pages 26 to 64 provide other opportunities to gather evidence for AF3.

Next steps for developing AF7

Provide further practice for developing children's vocabulary, for example:

- collect rhyming words and make class posters;
- make a simple rhyming dictionary (whole class activity);
- encourage children's interest in words by having a 'Word of the Day / Week'.

Task 1 on pages 9 to 16 and Tasks 5 and 6 on pages 47 to 64 provide other opportunites to gather evidence for AF7.

Task 3 Too Much Searching

Aims of this task

This task helps you to make judgements about children's attainment in Reading **AF2, AF4** and **AF7** (with opportunities to assess AF1, AF3 and AF6 as well) and Writing **AF2, AF3** and **AF4** (with opportunities to assess AF1 and AF8 as well). The children read and respond to a traditional African tale with a lesson to teach. They plan their own story and write the first paragraph.

Related Renewed Framework unit

Narrative Unit 2: Myths, legends, fables and traditional tales

Renewed Framework objectives

7.1, 7.4, 8.3, 9.4, 10.2

Key concepts

Reading

- identify the main events in the story, referring to the text to support their answers (AF2)
- explain what is important to characters in the story (AF3)
- recognise the cyclic structure of the story (AF4)
- understand the lesson the story teaches (AF6)
- find clues to the African setting in the story (AF7)

Writing

- name a setting and characters for a new story based on *Too Much Searching* (AF2)
- plan a parable with a cyclic structure, using the text as a model (AF3)
- construct a first paragraph for their story and use connective words within it (AF4)

Questions for guided reading

Starting off

Tell the children that they are going to read a parable. Have they read or heard any other parables? Explain that a parable is a type of fable: a story that has a moral or teaches a lesson. Tell the children that the story is from Africa and ask them to look for clues that show this as they read. Read the poem (AF1).

Read and respond

After reading, check that the children have understood the story by asking the following questions:

- **What clues did you find in the story to tell you that it is set in Africa? (AF7)**
- **How did the villagers know there was something wrong? (AF2)**
- **How did they work out what had happened? (AF2)**
- **What are the main events of the story in the order they happened? (AF2)**

Going deeper

- **Describe the pattern of the story. (AF4)**
- **Explain in your own words the lesson this story teaches. (AF6)**
- **What is a proverb? (AF3, AF7)**
- **Why do you think the proverb is set out differently from the rest of the story? (AF4)**
- **What does the story tell us about what the villagers thought was important? (AF3)**

Reflect

Discuss with the children whether or not it was the woodcutter's fault that the hunter died and how they feel towards the woodcutter, the hunter and the villagers. (AF6)

Task 3 Too Much Searching

A man went into the bush to cut wood. He passed many fine trees, but kept looking for a better one. Then he saw the tree he wanted on a high crag. He climbed to the top but saw that there was a rock where he wanted to stand. So he rolled it away and cut down the tree.

The rock rolled down into some bushes where an antelope lay. The frightened antelope jumped up and ran into some other bushes where a buffalo lay.

The buffalo thought it was being attacked and looked for its enemy. It saw a hunter walking past, charged at him and killed him. Vultures came and hovered over the hunter's body.

People in the village wondered why the vultures were hovering and went to see. They found the dead hunter and asked, "What made him die?"

They saw the buffalo's hoofprints and followed them to the bushes. "What made the buffalo run out of here?" they asked. Then they saw the antelope's hoofprints. They said, "An antelope ran in and surprised the buffalo. But what made the antelope run?"

Task 3 Too Much Searching

They followed the antelope's hoofprints to the other bushes and said, "Yes, the antelope came from here. But what made it run out?"

Then they found the rock and saw where it had rolled down the hill. They said, "The rock startled the antelope, but what made the rock roll down here?"

They followed the marks the rock had made as it rolled down the hill. At the top they came to the tree stump. "A man cut the tree down. The rock was in the way so he pushed it away and it rolled down the hill," they said.

Then they went home. They discussed everything and said, "When the sun rose all was quiet in the land. The man went to cut wood. He passed many fine trees but he wanted a better one. Everything would have stayed quiet but he climbed the crag. He moved the rock. He disturbed things that were lying quietly. So one thing happened, then another and the hunter died."

They made a proverb:

**"Too much searching disturbs things
that are lying still."**

Adaptation of original story by Harold Courlander

Task 3 Too Much Searching

1. List some things in the story that tell you it is set in Africa.

2. How did the villagers know there was something wrong?

3. How did they work out what had happened?

4. Write the main events of the story on the flow-chart in the order they happened.

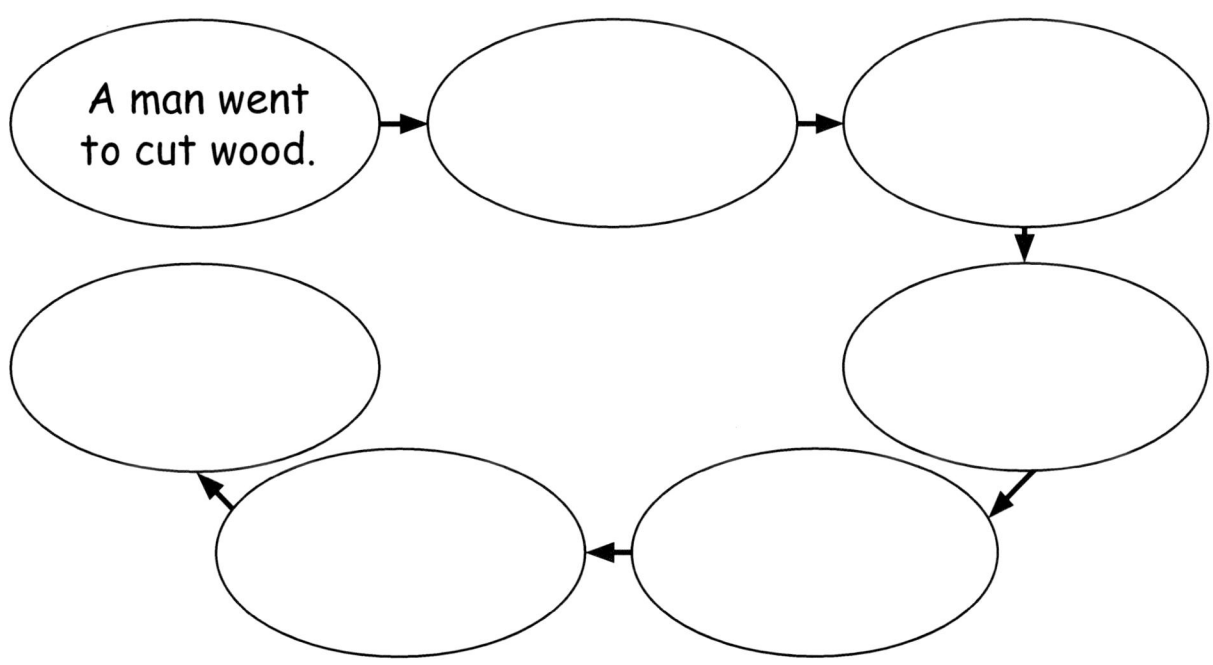

A man went to cut wood.

Task 3 Too Much Searching

5. Describe the pattern of the story.

6. Explain in your own words the lesson this story teaches.

7. Why do you think the proverb is set out differently from the rest of the story?

8. What does the story tell us about what the villagers thought was important?

Task 3 Too Much Searching

Main Assessment Focus: AF2 (understand, describe, select or retrieve information, events or ideas from texts and use quotation and reference to text)

Question	Exemplified responses	Grid reference	Notes
How did the villagers know there was something wrong?	Specific straightforward information: 'They saw the hovering vultures.'	Level 2 / bullet 1	
	Comments refer to text: 'It says they saw vultures and went to see.'	Level 3 / bullet 2	
How did they work out what had happened?	Straightforward information recalled: 'They saw the vultures hovering.'	Level 2 / bullet 1	
	Comments refer to text: 'They found the hunter, then they followed the hoofprints…'	Level 3 / bullet 2	
Write the main events of the story on the flow-chart in the order they happened.	Some main events recalled: what characters did, not all in correct order.	Level 2 / bullet 1	
	Main events recalled, might refer to text. Events in the correct order.	Level 3 / bullet 2	

Main Assessment Focus: AF4 (identify and comment on the structure and organisation of texts, including grammatical and presentational features at text level)

Question	Exemplified responses	Grid reference	Notes
Describe the pattern of the story.	Knows story is a series of events.	Level 2	
	Notes that story moves from place to place, ends up back at start – a cycle.	Level 3	
Why do you think the proverb is set out differently from the rest of the story?	Describes rather than explains: 'The letters are bigger / darker.'	Level 2	
	Simple explanation: 'It is in big letters because it is important'; 'Because it is the lesson of the story'.	Level 3	

Main Assessment Focus: AF7 (relate texts to their social, cultural and historical traditions)

Question	Exemplified responses	Grid reference	Notes
List some things in the story that tell you it is set in Africa.	Lists a few details that show that setting is not in UK.	Level 2 / bullet 1	
	Knows that story is set in Africa. Points out the animals that live in Africa.	Level 3 / bullet 1	

Other Assessment Focus: AF3 (deduce, infer or interpret information, events or ideas from texts)

Question	Exemplified responses	Grid reference	Notes
What does the story tell us about what the villagers thought was important?	Literal comment, sometimes misunderstanding story's message: 'Trees.'	Level 2 / bullet 2	
	Meaning established at literal level: 'Leave rocks alone, leave trees alone…'	Level 3 / bullet 2	

Other Assessment Focus: AF6 (identify and comment on writers' purposes and viewpoints, and the overall effect of the text on the reader)

Question	Exemplified responses	Grid reference	Notes
Explain in your own words the lesson the story teaches.	Explanation relates to story but might not be accurate: 'You shouldn't cut trees down.'	Level 2 / bullet 1	
	Uses some words directly from proverb but changes some: 'You shouldn't disturb things. You should let them lie still.'	Level 3 / bullet 1	

Exemplified responses matched to levels of attainment are provided as a guide. As always, professional judgement must be used when assessing pupils' learning progression and a range of evidence should be gathered for each AF.

Task 3 Too Much Searching

Think up your own story, with a lesson to teach.

1. Who is the story about?

....

....

2. What is the setting?

....

....

3. What lesson does your story teach?

....

....

4. List the main events of your story in the flow-chart.

REMEMBER! Something happens that makes something else happen and that makes something else happen and so on.

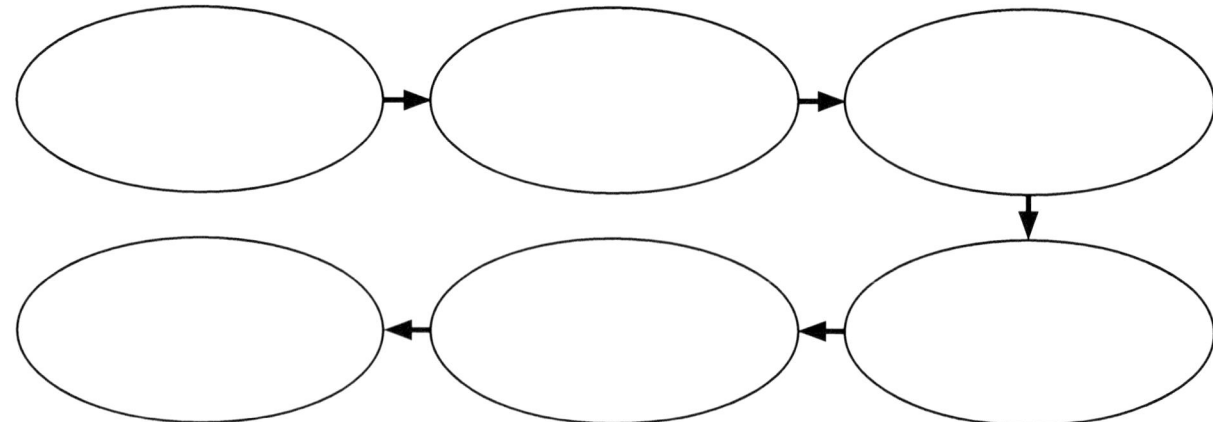

5. Now write the first paragraph of your story on a separate sheet of paper.

REMEMBER! Think about words for joining the sentences.

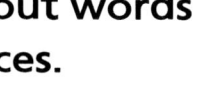  

Task 3 Too Much Searching

A pupil response within the range for Level 2 might be:

Questions 1 and 2 (AF2)

- Names the characters and gives an idea about who they are (animal, girl or boy, age, etc). Brief idea of setting: e.g. school, town, village.

Question 3 (AF2)

- An attempt to set out the message of the story but this might not be expressed in the 'statement' form of a proverb – possibly a past-tense summary of the story with an explanation, using 'because'.

Question 4 (AF3)

- Uses flow-chart to list events, showing some idea of chronological order (e.g. beginning and perhaps ending, with other parts out of sequence). Might write sentences rather than a heading or summary.

Question 5 (AF1, AF2, AF3, AF4, AF8)

AF1

Mostly relevant content although sparse: Sam the deer disobeys his mother and as a result is run over.

AF2

Uses feature of a story opening: 'One day…'.

Attempts to use story language: 'One day'.

Attempts appropriate style: there is a consequence to the deer's disobedience, but the 'lesson' is implied rather than made clear, except in the title.

> deer Never Cross The Road
> One day a ~~deer~~ called Sam wanted
> to go to his friends house.
> But his Mum would not let him
> go across the road on his own.
> Sam ran in to the road and
> a lorry hit him. The lorry driver
> headed to the hospital.
>
> C

AF3

Some basic sequencing of ideas achieved through the sequencing of sentences.

Only one time-related phrase: one day (signals opening).

AF4

Ideas in sequence with some connectives and pronouns used to link them: 'his', 'but', 'him'.

AF8

Correct spelling of some high-frequency grammatical function words: 'his', 'would', 'across'.

Also single morpheme context / lexical words: 'deer', 'friend', 'house', 'road', 'lorry', 'driver'.

Task 3 Too Much Searching

A pupil response within the range for Level 3 might be:

Questions 1 and 2 (AF2)

- Shows some link between the characters and setting: e.g. if set in a school, children, teachers.

Question 3 (AF2)

- Story message presented as a simple statement: e.g. if you do wrong you get found out.

Question 4 (AF3)

- An attempt to summarise main events or give them headings. Some headings / summaries have clear links to others in sequence.

Question 5 (AF1, AF2, AF3, AF4, AF8)

AF1

Appropriate content: animal in danger.

Attempts to elaborate with adjectives: 'horrid', 'scared', 'frightened'.

Explains background: Mike had been looking for Fluffy for a long time, he might make a rabbit pie with her.

Attempts to adopt a viewpoint: Mike was a horrid man.

AF2

Main features of the story opening used: opens with 'a week ago' and provides background before narrating the story.

Appropriate style used: past tenses, beginning.

'Lesson' is implied, rather than explicit: animals should beware of some humans.

AF3

Some attempt to sequence: begins with 'a week ago', uses 'had been' to indicate events that happened before the present story begins.

Opening signalled: 'A week ago', ending signalled: 'They all gave up'.

Be kind to other people

A week ago there was a rabbit called Flugy who needed
help getting out of a trap. It was Set by a man called
Mike. Mike was a horrid man. He had been looking
for Flugy for a long time. She was verey sceard because
She was pritend that Mike might kill her and make
a rabbit pie. She asked all the humens to help.
They tried to break the rope but the could not, So Flugy
asked the animals. They tried but they sould not even
brak it. They all gave up.

AF8

Mainly correct spelling of high-frequency grammatical function words: 'ago', 'because', 'could', 'even' (but not 'very').

Mainly correct spelling of common content / lexical words with more than one morpheme: 'rabbit', 'horrid', 'humans', 'animals'.

Errors: inflected endings ('fritend').

Plausible phonetic attempts at content / lexical words: 'sceard' (like 'heard'), 'frite'.

AF4

Uses adverbial: 'a week ago'.

Pronouns used to link sentences: 'who', 'it', 'he', 'she', 'they'.

Task 3 Too Much Searching

Reading

Next steps for developing AF2

To develop the children's skills in understanding, describing and retrieving information, events or ideas from texts, you could introduce discussion points such as the following when reading a text together:

- How can you tell where this story is set / when it happened? Which words and phrases in the text are clues?
- Who are the main characters? What is their relationship to each other?
- What was the first key event in the story? What else happened because of this?

This activity should be part of a range of evidence gathered for AF2. Evidence for AF2 can be gathered from other sources, such as:

- observations during guided and shared reading;
- drama activities such as recreating a story, freeze framing;
- creating story maps;
- research in other subject areas, e.g. finding information in geography.

All tasks in this book provide opportunities to gather evidence for AF2.

Next steps for developing AF4

Children will benefit from further practice in identifying and commenting on the structure and organisation of texts, using questions and prompts such as:

- Tell the beginning / middle / end of the story.
- How does the writer show us that there is a change in time / place?
- Why has the writer used capital letters / bold text / italics / headings / bullet points?

This activity should be part of a range of evidence gathered for AF4. Evidence for AF4 can also be gathered from other sources, such as:

- observations during guided and shared reading;
- story-sequencing activities;
- text annotations of organisational and presentational features;
- discussion of different text features (e.g. headings, diagrams, index, captions) following research in other curriculum subjects.

Task 2 on pages 17 to 25, Task 4 on pages 37 to 46, Task 5 on pages 47 to 55 and Task 6 on pages 56 to 64 provide other opportunities to gather evidence for AF4.

Next steps for developing AF7

You could develop children's understanding of the way in which texts reflect social, cultural and historical traditions through questions and discussion points such as:

- What do you know about [the place where this story is set]?
- What do you think was happening there at that time?
- How might the story change in a different setting (place or time)?
- How do people's beliefs affect what happened?

This activity should be part of a range of evidence gathered for AF7. Evidence for AF7 can also be gathered from other sources, such as:

- reading and responding to other traditional stories and stories from other cultures;
- investigating local and national folklore;
- watching and discussing dramas and films set in different times and places or which reflect the beliefs or attitudes of a different community.

Task 3 Too Much Searching

Writing

Next steps for developing AF2

You could help children to think about the intended reader of their writing through discussion points and questions such as:

- Who are you writing for?
- How would you change it for a younger child to read?
- How will you make them want to read on?

This should be part of a range of writing activities from which evidence is gathered for AF2. Evidence for AF2 can also be gathered from:

- writing other genres of narrative text for specific audiences, e.g. a retelling of a traditional tale for a younger brother or sister;
- writing non-fiction texts, e.g. instructions for a specific group of people.

Task 2 on pages 17 to 25, Task 4 on pages 37 to 46 and Task 6 on pages 56 to 64 provide other opportunities to gather evidence for AF2.

Next steps for developing AF3

You could develop the children's understanding of how to organise and present stories through questions and activities such as:

- How did you begin… [a chapter or paragraph]? How does it set the scene for a story? How does it link to the chapter / paragraph before?
- Listing the key events in their or a partner's story or chapter in the correct order, perhaps as a flow-chart.
- How did you end your story, and why? What would the reader think or wonder?

This should be part of a range of writing activities from which evidence is gathered for AF3. Evidence for AF3 can also be gathered from:

- planning, organising and writing other genres of narrative text;
- planning, organising and writing playscripts and poetry;
- planning, organising and writing non-fiction texts, especially information texts and non-chronological reports.

Task 2 on pages 17 to 25, Task 4 on pages 37 to 46, Task 5 on pages 47 to 55 and Task 6 on pages 56 to 64 provide other opportunities to gather evidence for AF3.

Next steps for developing AF4

You could develop the children's skills in constructing paragraphs and linking their ideas through activities, questions and discussion points such as:

- Writing the main events or main ideas of the paragraph on slips of paper and arranging them in an appropriate order;
- Writing key words for the main ideas or events on a mind map and then joining them with lines on which they write sentences to link them;
- Replacing nouns in sentences with pronouns, and recognising where a pronoun should not be used (for example, if it is not clear which noun it refers to).

This should be part of a range of writing activities from which evidence is gathered for AF4. Evidence for AF4 can also be gathered from:

- paragraphs the children write in other fiction genres such as an adventure or mystery story;
- letters they write to find information or to thank visitors to the school.

You could also use the children's work from some of the other writing tasks in this book to assess AF4, although they are designed mainly to focus on other AFs.

Task 4 How to Recycle Paper

Aims of this task

This task will help you to make judgements about children's attainment in Reading **AF2, AF3** and **AF4** (with opportunities to assess AF5 and AF6 as well) and Writing **AF2, AF3** and **AF6** (with opportunity to assess AF8 as well). The children read and respond to a non-fiction instructional text about how to make recycled paper. They plan and write their own set of instructions.

Related Renewed Framework unit

Non-fiction Unit 2: Instructions

Renewed Framework objectives

7.2, 7.3, 9.3, 9.4, 10.2, 11.2

Key concepts

Reading

- find specific information in instructions (AF2)
- deduce why particular equipment is needed (AF3)
- identify and explain features of layout, text and illustrations in instructions (AF4)
- comment on the form of verbs and their position in instruction sentences (AF5)
- identify and comment on intended audience for instructions (AF6)

Writing

- write simple instructions for other children of their own age to follow (AF2)
- draw and write a plan for a set of instructions (AF3)
- write verbs in the instruction (imperative) form (AF6)

Questions for guided reading

Starting off

Ask the children what instructions are for. They could give examples. You could play 'Simon Says' to remind them of instruction sentences. Then let them read the heading. Ask them what they think they will find out from these instructions.

Read and respond

Ask the children to read the instructions and to notice how instructions are different from fiction texts. Ask them the following questions to assess their understanding:

- **What equipment do you need to make recycled paper? (AF2)**
- **What materials is the paper made from? (AF2)**
- **Why are the things you need set out first, in a list? (AF4)**
- **Why are the instructions split into stages? (AF4)**
- How are bullet points helpful? (AF4)
- **What do you notice about the verbs in each sentence? (AF5)**

Going deeper

- **Who are the instructions written for? (AF6)**
- **Why do you need a pair of tights? (AF3)**
- **Why should you leave the mixture for a week at the end of Stage 1? (AF3)**

Reflect

Discuss other differences between instruction sentences and sentences in a story. The children could comment on the length of the sentences. Ask why instruction sentences are short. (AF4)

Task 4 How to Recycle Paper

How to Make Recycled Paper

You will need
Old paper
Bucket
Water
Paper towel
Newspaper
Plastic lid (such as an ice-cream tub)
Pair of tights

Stage 1
- Rip the paper into small pieces.
- Put the paper in a bucket with water.
- Stir the small pieces in the bucket.
- Squash it with your hands.
- Leave it for a week.

Stage 2
- Make holes in a plastic lid to make a sieve.
- Stretch a pair of tights over the sieve.
- Pour the contents of the bucket through the sieve.
- Leave it for about a minute.

Stage 3
- Get the paper towel and newspaper.
- Flip the mixture onto the paper towel and newspaper.
- Press the paper towel on the mixture.
- Leave your recycled paper to dry.

Task 4 How to Recycle Paper

1. What equipment do you need to make recycled paper?

2. What materials are used to make the paper?

3. Why are the things you need set out first, in a list?

4. Why are the instructions split into stages?

Task 4 How to Recycle Paper

5. What do you notice about the verbs in each sentence? Give examples.

6. Why do you need a pair of tights?

7. Why should you leave the mixture for a week at the end of Stage 1?

8. Who are the instructions written for?

Task 4 How to Recycle Paper

Main Assessment Focus: AF2 (understand, describe, select or retrieve information, events or ideas from texts and use quotation and reference to text)

Question	Exemplified responses	Grid reference	Notes
What equipment do you need to make recycled paper?	Names equipment; might include materials. Might not use 'You will need' list.	Level 2 / bullet 1	
	Some distinction between equipment and materials. Uses 'You will need' list.	Level 3 / bullet 2	
What materials is the paper made from?	Includes some materials; unclear about distinction between materials and equipment.	Level 2 / bullet 1	
	Names materials in list. Checks text to find which ones are made into paper.	Level 3 / bullet 2	

Main Assessment Focus: AF3 (deduce, infer or interpret information, events or ideas from texts)

Question	Exemplified responses	Grid reference	Notes
Why do you need a pair of tights?	Simple comment based on text reference: 'To make a sieve'.	Level 2 / bullet 2	
	Interprets text information: 'To go over the sieve so that only the water goes through.'	Level 3 / bullet 2	
Why should you leave the mixture for a week at the end of Stage 1?	Simple reference back to text: 'Because you have finished Stage 1.'	Level 2 / bullet 1	
	Inference based on text reference: 'It says "Put the paper in water" so it needs to soak.'	Level 3 / bullet 1	

Main Assessment Focus: AF4 (identify and comment on the structure and organisation of texts, including grammatical and presentational features at text level)

Question	Exemplified responses	Grid reference	Notes
Why are the things you need set out first, in a list?	Some awareness of features: 'So you will see them.'	Level 2	
	Basic features with linked comment: 'It stands out so you can get everything ready before you start.'	Level 3	
Why are the instructions split into stages?	Response at simple level: 'To split them up.'	Level 2	
	Awareness of instruction features: 'They are in order. You do 1 then 2 then 3.'	Level 3	

Other Assessment Focus: AF5 (explain and comment on writers' use of language, including grammatical and literary features at word and sentence level)

Question	Exemplified responses	Grid reference	Notes
What do you notice about the verbs in each sentence?	Identifies verbs but not position. Verb form implied: 'Rip is a verb. It says what you do.'	Level 2 / bullet 2	
	Notes position and that they 'sound like instructions'. Might comment on present tense.	Level 3	

Other Assessment Focus: AF6 (identify and comment on writers' purposes and viewpoints, and the overall effect of the text on the reader)

Question	Exemplified responses	Grid reference	Notes
Who are the instructions written for?	Some idea of purpose and audience: 'People read them to find out what to do.'	Level 2 / bullet 1	
	Identifies audience, using text and illustration, but with no explanation: 'Someone who wants to make recycled paper – for children.'	Level 3 / bullet 1	

Exemplified responses matched to levels of attainment are provided as a guide. As always, professional judgement must be used when assessing pupils' learning progression and a range of evidence should be gathered for each AF.

Task 4 How to Recycle Paper

1. Write three sentences to tell someone how to fill a glass of water.

   Remember! Start each sentence with a verb.

   • ....

     ....

   • ....

     ....

   • ....

     ....

2. Plan instruction text for something you know how to do or make – such as making a sandwich or washing the dishes.

3. On another piece of paper write your instructions for someone else of your age.

   REMEMBER!

   • Write a list of things you need.

   • Make sure your instructions are in order.

Task 4 How to Recycle Paper

A pupil response within the range for Level 2 might be:

Question 1 (AF6)

- Sentences make sense, most begin with capital letters and end with full stops. They might not all be in the imperative form.

Question 2 (AF3)

- Some basic organisation evident in plan, e.g. a separate list of materials, boxes for pictures. Might begin to write instructions rather than headings.

Question 3 (AF2, AF3, AF6, AF8)

AF2

Some basic purpose established: main features of instructions (list of items needed, followed by instructions).

Some attempts to adopt appropriate style: use of imperative verbs, with verbs near the beginning of the sentence.

AF3

Some basic sequencing of ideas: line break between each instruction; bullet point to begin each instruction in sequence.

The order of the instructions makes sense but some items and instructions are missing: e.g. spread duvet on bed; put pillowcases on pillows and put these on bed.

Time-related words in sequence: first, then, next.

AF6

Clause structure grammatically correct: e.g. 'First get a clean mattress', '...put the duvet neatly inside the cover'.

Correct demarcation of sentences using capital letters and full stops.

AF8

Correct spelling of high-frequency grammatical function words: 'get', 'and', 'then'.

Errors with inflected endings: 'makeing'.

Phonetic attempts at vowel digraphs: 'cleen', 'doovay' (duvet).

Makeing a bed.

- First you will need
  a mattress
  a dooray
  a sheet
  a cover

- First get a cleen mattress and put it on the bed.

- Then get a ~~sh~~ sheet and put it ontop of the mattress on the bed.

- ~~Nexst~~ Next get a cleen dooray.

- Then get a cover and put the dooray neatly inside the cover.

Task 4 How to Recycle Paper

A pupil response within the range for Level 3 might be:

Question 1 (AF6)

- Sentences make sense, begin with capital letters and end with full stops. Most are in the imperative form with the verb at the beginning.

Question 2 (AF3)

- Plan shows a box or other demarcated area for materials. One or more of the following included: lines, bullet points, numbers or other signal for each instruction and box for illustration. Headings indicating content.

Question 3 (AF2, AF3, AF6, AF8)

AF2

Purpose established at a general level: heading 'How to make a cup of tea'.

Main features of instructions / recipes used: list of materials and equipment (although some are missing) with heading 'What you need', followed by numbered instructions.

Attempt at appropriate style: use of imperative verbs; attention to reader ('if you want it', 'stir as long as you like', 'if you like it sweet', 'if you want').

AF3

Some attempt to organise ideas: use of numbering to establish order of actions, with related points next to one another ('get a cup', 'put a teabag in the cup'; 'put it [kettle] on', 'when the water has boiled'.) Thus ideas are sequenced logically.

The crossing out of bullet points and replacing them with numbers indicates thought about the best way of signalling the sequence.

AF6

Straightforward sentences demarcated with full stops and capital letters (no question or exclamation marks needed).

AF8

Correct spelling of more difficult grammatical function words: 'how', 'what', 'some'.

Errors in more difficult inflected endings: 'bolded' (boiled), 'pord' (poured).

Phonetically plausible attempts at content / lexical words: 'suger', 'strer' (stir).

How to make a cup of tea

What you need

A tea bag
Some milk
Some hot water
Suger (if you want it)
A pair of hands

1. Firts get a cup out.
2. Then get a tea bag and put it in the cup.
3. Next put some water in the kettle and put it on.
4. Then get the milk out of the fridge.
5. When the kettle has bolded pord pord it into a cup up to the middle.
6. Then get the milk and pord into the cup and fill the cup up.
7. And strer as long as you like.
8. If you like it sweet put some suger in if you want.

Task 4 How to Recycle Paper

Reading

Next steps for developing AF2

To further develop the children's skills in understanding, describing and retrieving information, events or ideas from texts, you could use questions such as the following when reading instructional text together:

- What equipment do you need for making...?
- What materials do you need for making...?
- Why do you need...? Point out the words that tell you this.
- Which parts might be tricky to do? Why? Which words tell you this?

This activity should be part of a range of evidence gathered for AF2. Evidence for AF2 related to instructional and non-fiction texts can be gathered from other sources, such as:

- following instructions that have been read or from a television programme or website;
- research and note-making for other subjects: e.g. geography, science, history.

All tasks in the book provide opportunities to gather evidence for AF2.

Next steps for developing AF3

Children will benefit from further practice in answering inferential questions and using reference to the text to support answers. When reading instructional text, ask:

- What would happen if you did [Stage 1] before [Stage 2]?
- Why do you think you need [a piece of equipment]?
- How do the pictures / diagrams help? What information do they add?

This activity should be part of a range of evidence gathered for AF3. Evidence for AF3 can be gathered from a range of sources, such as:

- observations during guided and shared reading;
- comparing different types of instructional texts;
- reading and following instructions in other curriculum areas.

Task 1 on pages 7 to 16 and Task 3 on pages 26 to 36 provide other opportunities to gather evidence for AF3.

Next steps for developing AF4

You could develop the children's understanding of the structure and organisation of instructions through questions and discussion points such as:

- How does the layout help you to understand the instructions and follow them?
- What features have been used to show the order of the steps?
- How do the pictures and diagrams help?

This activity should be part of a range of evidence gathered for AF4. Evidence for AF4 can also be gathered from other sources, such as:

- observations during guided and shared reading of instructions and other non-fiction texts;
- identifying and commenting on features of different types of non-fiction texts connected with different areas of the curriculum;
- evaluating instructional texts, including those written by children: e.g. in design and technology.

Task 2 on pages 17 to 25, Task 3 on pages 26 to 36, Task 5 on pages 47 to 55 and Task 6 pages 56 to 64 provide other opportunities to gather evidence for AF4.

Task 4 How to Recycle Paper

Writing

Next steps for developing AF2

You could help children to think about the intended reader of their writing through discussion points and questions such as:

- Who are you writing the instructions for?
- What do they need to know?
- Do any items or actions need explaining?
- How would you change it for a different reader: e.g. a younger child or an alien?

This should be part of a range of writing activities from which evidence is gathered for AF2. Evidence for AF2 can also be gathered from:

- non-fiction writing in other subjects: e.g. recording information or writing reports in science, geography or history;
- writing letters that use language appropriate for the reader and purpose.

Task 2 on pages 17 to 25, Task 3 on pages 26 to 36 and Task 6 on pages 56 to 64 provide other opportunities to gather evidence for AF2.

Next steps for developing AF3

You could develop the children's understanding of how to organise and present instructions through discussion points and activities such as:

- Enacting / miming the process they are going to write instructions for, while others list the main actions and any equipment or materials.
- Selecting instructions for trialling by someone else. What problems did they face following the instructions?
- Writing recounts of artefacts they have made and then converting them to instructions.

This should be part of a range of writing activities from which evidence is gathered for AF3. Evidence for AF3 can also be gathered from:

- planning, organising and writing letters, reports and information texts;
- planning, organising and writing poetry;
- planning, organising and writing narrative texts, considering time sequencing.

Task 2 on pages 17 to 25, Task 3 on pages 26 to 36, Task 5 on pages 47 to 55 and Task 6 on pages 56 to 64 provide other opportunities to gather evidence for AF3.

Next steps for developing AF6

You could develop the children's understanding of syntax, punctuation and sentence structure through activities, discussion and questioning such as:

- Changing verbs from present to past tense and vice versa.
- Converting recount sentences about something the children have made into instruction sentences, focusing on the form of the verb and its position in the sentence.
- Peer marking to simplify and shorten sentences, deleting unnecessary words and then justifying the deletions.

This should be part of a range of writing activities from which evidence is gathered for AF6. Evidence for AF6 can also be gathered from:

- narrative or reports that features complex sentences;
- narrative or other non-fiction writing that includes phrases and clauses linked by time or logical connectives;
- narrative or other non-fiction writing that includes the use of exclamations, questions and sentences with commas and dialogue.

Task 1 on pages 7 to 16 and Task 6 on pages 48 to 56 provide other opportunities to gather evidence for AF6.

Task 5 Flood!

Aims of this task

This task is designed to help you to make judgements about children's attainment in Reading **AF2** and **AF4** (with opportunities to assess AF1 and AF5 as well) and Writing **AF3, AF5** and **AF7** (with opportunity to assess AF1 as well). The children read and respond to the first two chapters of an adventure story written by two eight-year-olds. They write a cliff-hanger ending for the next chapter.

Related Renewed Framework unit

Narrative Unit 3: Adventure and mystery

Renewed Framework objectives

7.1, 9.1, 9.2, 9.4, 10.1, 11.1

Key concepts

Reading
- retrieve information about background to the story and the main events (AF2)
- identify the use of a cliff-hanger as a structural device (AF4)
- comment on how the writers' language helps the reader to imagine a scene (AF5)

Writing
- plan the next chapter and write a cliff-hanger ending for it (AF1, AF3)
- use varied sentences for effect (AF5)
- write interesting words / phrases that show the passage of time (AF7)

Questions for guided reading

Starting off

Tell the children they are going to read two chapters from a long story written by two eight-year-olds. As they read it, they should look at how each of the two chapters develops the plot and how the writers help the reader to imagine the sights, sounds and action. Introduce the term 'cliff-hanger'. The children might be able to give examples from serial television programmes they have watched.

Read and respond

Read the text (AF1) and then use the following questions to prompt discussion:
- **What do you find out in Chapter 1? (AF2)**
- **Why did the writers end Chapter 1 with the Head telling everyone they are marooned? (AF4)**
- **What are the main events of Chapter 2? (AF2)**
- **Which words and phrases help readers to imagine the scenes in the story? (AF5)**

Going deeper
- **What does the first paragraph of Chapter 2 do? (AF4)**
- What does the second chapter do? (AF4)
- Which words and phrases show the passage of time in the story? How are these useful in building up the story? (AF5)

Reflect

What might happen in Chapter 3? (AF3)

Task 5 Flood! by Jakk and Ranjit, aged 8

Chapter 1: Marooned!

There had been waterworks on Earlham Road for over a month now!

It took the children a long time to get home. Steve, Jamie and Sam were sick of it.

"I wonder how long this will go on for?" wondered Sam.

Jamie and Steve wondered too.

"It's probably going to take five weeks," said Sam.

The next day the three boys walked to school together. Suddenly they heard a shout from near the roadworks: "HELP!"

They saw water pouring out from the roadworks. So they ran for their lives all the way to school.

They burst through the classroom door shouting, "FLOOD!"

"Then shut the door!" ordered Charlotte, and so they did.

The Head walked in and said, "I'm sorry children, we are marooned for a month."

Chapter 2: The Worst Lunch Ever

It was quarter past twelve, lunchtime! Sam sat down and waited for his hot lunch. He waited for five minutes until the Head came in and said: "I'm sorry children, there are no hot dinners today because the dinner couldn't arrive through the flood."

Everyone sighed, but mostly Sam. "I wonder what we're going to eat," Sam wondered.

He went to Jamie and Steve and sighed. "Can you believe it? No hot lunches!"

Meanwhile the water was still rising.

Suddenly there was a shout. "Come quick!" It was Charlotte.

The three of them rushed to the door, but they had to wait ten minutes before it was their turn to go and look at the water. It was rising fast. Steve, Jamie and Sam stood at the door staring at the glittering, giant puddle of dirty water. Suddenly the water crept through a crack in the door. A shiver ran down their spines. They were frightened.

Task 5 Flood!

1. What do you find out in Chapter 1?

2. Why did the writers end Chapter 1 with the Head telling everyone that they are marooned?

3. What are the main events of Chapter 2?

flood!

4. Which words and phrases help readers to imagine the scenes in the story?

5. What does the first paragraph of Chapter 2 do?

Task 5 Flood!

Main Assessment Focus: AF2 (understand, describe, select or retrieve information, events or ideas from texts and use quotation and reference to texts)

Question	Exemplified responses	Grid reference	Notes
What do you find out in Chapter 1?	Recalls some key events: 'There was a flood; the children ran into school; they shut the door.'	Level 2 / bullet 1	
	Recalls main events, characters and setting but with no specific detail: 'There were roadworks near the school; Water escaped and there was a flood; The worker shouted "Help"; The Head said that they were marooned.'	Level 3 / bullet 1	
What are the main events of Chapter 2?	Simple response about events: 'They had lunch and they ran to look at the water that came in.'	Level 2 / bullet 1	
	Identifies main events: 'It was lunchtime; the flood water was creeping under the door.' Might start re-telling: 'Charlotte shouted "Come quick!" and water came under the door.'	Level 3 / bullet 1	

Main Assessment Focus: AF4 (identify and comment on the structure and organisation of texts, including grammatical and presentational features at text level)

Question	Exemplified responses	Grid reference	Notes
Why did the writers end this chapter with the Head telling everyone they are marooned?	Personal or literal response: 'So they could tell their mum or dad'; 'So they wouldn't get wet or drown'; 'The next chapter says what happened next.'	Level 2	
	Some awareness of the use of the 'cliff-hanger': 'So you'll want to read the next chapter to see what happens.'	Level 3	
What does the first paragraph of Chapter 2 do?	Awareness of time change, though not explicit: 'It is lunchtime. The children are waiting for their hot dinners.'	Level 2	
	Identifies it as a time change: 'It tells us that it is later on. It is now lunchtime.'	Level 3	

Other Assessment Focus: AF5 (explain and comment on writers' use of language, including grammatical and literary features at word and sentence level)

Question	Exemplified responses	Grid reference	Notes
Which words help readers to imagine the scenes in the story?	Identifies some effective words but with no comment: '"Burst" is a good word'; 'I like "marooned".'	Level 2 / bullet 1	
	Identifies basic features of language, with little or no comment: 'There are some good words for "said", like "shouting", "ordered" and "sighed"'; '"A shiver ran down their spines" shows they were scared.'	Level 3	

Exemplified responses matched to levels of attainment are provided as a guide. As always, professional judgement must be used when assessing pupils' learning progression and a range of evidence should be gathered for each AF.

Task 5 Flood!

1. Write some interesting words and phrases that can show the passage of time in a story.

2. Plan the next chapter of the story. Write notes about the main events.

Chapter 3

3. Write a cliff-hanger ending for Chapter 3. Use a separate piece of paper or the back of this sheet.

REMEMBER!

- Use interesting words to show the passage of time.

- Use some short and some longer sentences.

 Flood!

A pupil response within the range for Level 2 might be:

Question 1 (AF7)

- Some interesting words and phrases – using those from the text: e.g. a long time, suddenly, a quarter past twelve, five minutes, ten minutes.

Question 2 (AF3)

- New chapter shows links with the previous one. Characters from the stimulus text appear in the new chapter; there is more about the water coming under the door.

Question 3 (AF1, AF3, AF5, AF7)

AF1

Relevant content (e.g. rescuing belongings from the flood, getting on to the roof for safety), but rather repetitive speech ('get are things', 'get are belongings', 'get are penceil caseies', 'get are school bag').

Apt word choices: 'belongings' and, to indicate panic / response to emergency, 'quic'.

AF3

Some basic sequencing of ideas: time-related words and phrases ('first', 'second', 'third', 'then').

Closing signalled: chapter ends with a character wondering what will happen next.

AF5

Variation in sentence openings: 'quic', 'I wonder if', 'carefully'.

Mainly simple sentences.

Consistent use of past tense in narration and present tense in speech: 'So they did that', 'Then Charlotte started crying', 'Let's get are school bag', 'Why are you crying?'

AF7

Simple, speech-like vocabulary, limited in range: 'started crying', 'I miss my mum and dad'.

Some adventurous word choices: 'quic', 'carefully'.

> Flood! chapter 3.
>
> quic Sam said there's a ladder. No let's carefully get are belongings. good iade Charlotte .thanks Sam. first lets get are school bag, second let's get are penceil caseies, third let get are other things. ok and get en any thing warm ok charlotte? So we don't get ill yeah. So they did that. lets go on the roof. ok. I think I'm comeing down th with something! Then charlotte started crying. why are you crying? I miss my mum and Dad. It is ok charlotte I miss my my mum and Dad is well. you do? I wonder if are mum and dad will ever find again !!!!....

Task 5 Flood!

A pupil response within the range for Level 3 might be:

Question 1 (AF7)

- Simple vocabulary but some words and phrases chosen for effect: e.g. in a flash, at that moment.

Question 2 (AF3)

- Chapter 3 plan builds on Chapter 2. Some ideas about flood water, what the teacher and children do. Notes indicate some sequencing of events.

Question 3 (AF1, AF3, AF5, AF7)

AF1

Some imaginative and appropriate ideas: elaboration ('window in their class led up to', 'water started pushing the door open').

AF3

Ideas sequenced: 'water started pushing the door open', 'now the water was up to their knees'.

Also sequencing of children's actions: 'ran into their classroom corner', 'clambered up on top of the chairs and tables...'.

Closing signalled: 'I wonder if the flood will ever go down.'

Flood! Chapter 3.

Class 5 ran into their classroom corner too scared to move! "Help!" cryed Sam. Suddenly the water started pushing the door open! Everyone was terrified! Now the water was up to their knee's! "What's happening and how will we get out of here?" Said Steve who had just swallowed some of the flooding water. He coughed and spluttered. "Oh dear, I don't want you getting a cough" Said the teacher. Then suddenly Jamie saw that the window in their class led up to the roof and it wasn't very high, so they clambered up on top of the chairs and tables up to the window and onto the roof. "I wonder if the flood will ever go down!" mumbled Jamie. Do you wonder too?

AF5

Mainly uses simply structured sentences: 'Suddenly the water started pushing the door open', 'Everyone was terrified'.

Some complex sentences, some subordination: '"What's happening and how will we get out of here?" said Steve who had just swallowed some of the flooding water.'

Some variation in use of past and present tenses: '"Oh dear. I don't want you getting a cough," said the teacher.'

AF7

Appropriate vocabulary selected: 'Everyone was terrified', 'Now the water was up to their knees'.

Some words selected for effect: 'too scared to move', 'coughed and spluttered', 'clambered'.

Task 5 Flood!

Reading

Next steps for developing AF2

To further develop the children's skills in understanding, describing and retrieving information, events or ideas from texts, you could ask questions such as the following when reading a text together:

- Why don't [character x] and [character y] get on with one another?
- Why wouldn't [character x]…? Which words tell you this?
- What are the key events of this chapter? Point out where each one begins.
- Which event changes what happens in the story?

This activity should be part of a range of evidence gathered for AF2. Evidence for AF2 can be gathered from other sources, such as:

- reading and responding to both fiction and non-fiction texts, in print and other media;
- drama activities – e.g. role-play, acting out stories;
- note-making for other subjects: e.g. geography, science, history.

All tasks in this book provide opportunities to gather evidence for AF2.

Next steps for developing AF4

You could develop the children's understanding of the structure and organisation of stories through discussion points and questions such as:

- Why does chapter x end as it does (e.g. cliff-hanger, question, warning)?
- Explain the author's use of chapter headings.
- What do the illustrations add to your understanding of the text?
- How does the writer set the scene / provide information about characters or what has already happened before the story begins?

This activity should be part of a range of evidence gathered for AF4. Evidence for AF4 can also be gathered from other sources, such as:

- observations during guided and shared reading of different genres of text;
- investigating the organisation of different types of text, especially when text is suited to its purpose: e.g. explanations with diagrams; alphabetically-ordered information, such as a glossary, index or dictionary; on-screen texts.

Task 2 on pages 17 to 25, Task 3 on pages 26 to 36, Task 4 on pages 37 to 46 and Task 6 on pages 56 to 64 provide other opportunities to gather evidence for AF4.

Writing

Next steps for developing AF3

You could develop the children's understanding of how to organise and present stories through discussion points and activities such as:

- Looking at how they began a chapter or paragraph: how it sets the scene for a story or links to a previous chapter or paragraph.
- Asking questions about what could happen in the story: e.g. if flood water started coming into the school, what would the children do first? What would the teacher do? What would happen next?
- Listing the key events in their or a partner's story or chapter in the correct order, perhaps as a flow-chart.
- Discussing how they ended a chapter or story, and why. What would the reader think or wonder?

 Task 5 Flood!

Writing (continued)

Next steps for developing AF3

This should be part of a range of writing activities from which evidence is gathered for AF3. Evidence for AF3 can also be gathered from:

- planning, organising and writing other genres of narrative text;
- planning, organising and writing poetry;
- planning, organising and writing non-fiction texts.

Task 2 on pages 17 to 25, Task 3 on pages 26 to 36, Task 4 on pages 37 to 46 and Task 6 on pages 56 to 64 provide other opportunities to gather evidence for AF3.

Next steps for developing AF5

You could develop the children's skills in writing varying sentences to add interest and create effects in stories through discussion points and activities such as:

- Looking at the first words of each sentence and considering whether they are repetitive and whether this is appropriate for the story.
- Deciding whether any sentences could be extended, and how.
- Considering where any sentences would be better split into shorter sentences: e.g. 'What's happening and how will we get out of here?' or 'What's happening? How will we get out?'
- Considering the connective words in their sentences, whether they can be replaced with commas or different words.

This should be part of a range of writing activities from which evidence is gathered for AF5. Evidence for AF5 can also be gathered from:

- sentences the children write in other subjects, to communicate information, ideas or points of view;
- writing notes and then expanding them to create sentences;
- writing poetry (this could include splitting sentences across lines of poetry and writing words and phrases that do not form complete sentences).

You could also use the children's work from some of the other writing tasks in this book to assess AF5, although they are designed mainly to focus on other AFs.

Next steps for developing AF7

You could develop the children's vocabulary and their appreciation of the effects of words through activities and discussions such as:

- Picking out words from the children's writing and talking about their effects: e.g. 'suddenly', 'spluttered', 'clambered'.
- Asking if they can think of some better words for some of the ones they used: e.g. is 'suddenly' used too often? Is it always the best word? Perhaps consider 'all of a sudden', 'in a flash'.
- Enacting scenes, considering how a person spoke or moved then asking for words to express this and suggesting some: 'yelled', 'whispered', 'strode' etc.

This should be part of a range of writing activities from which evidence is gathered for AF7. Evidence for AF7 can also be gathered from:

- writing connected with topics the children have studied in other subjects;
- previous work on powerful or expressive verbs or adjectives.

Task 1 on pages 7 to 16, Task 2 on pages 17 to 25 and Task 6 on pages 56 to 64 provide other opportunities to gather evidence for AF7.

Task 6 Frogs and Toads

Aims of this task

This task is designed to help you to make judgements about children's attainment in Reading in **AF2**, **AF4** and **AF6** and Writing **AF1**, **AF2** and **AF3** (with opportunities to assess AF6 and AF7 as well). The children read and respond to a non-fiction information text about frogs and toads, in which the information is presented as a table. They write their own information text comparing two animals.

Related Renewed Framework unit

Non-fiction Unit 3: Information texts

Renewed Framework objectives

7.3, 9.1, 9.3, 9.4, 11.2

Key concepts

Reading

- select and retrieve basic information about frogs and toads (AF2)
- comment on and evaluate the format of the text (AF4)
- identify audience and purpose for text (AF6)

Writing

- choose relevant ideas and content for writing (AF1)
- create a 'Spot the difference' table for two other creatures (AF2, AF3)
- write questions to help someone to decide whether an animal is a frog or a toad, using correct punctuation and appropriate connectives (AF6)

Questions for guided reading

Starting off

Show the children the table and ask them if this is a fiction or non-fiction text, and how they can tell. Ask them to read it and, as they do so, to look at how it is organised and how this makes it easy to find information.

Read and respond

Ask the children what kinds of information they can find out from the text. How did they find that out quickly? Remind them that they don't need to read a whole text to find out what it is about, but can scan it for headings, pictures, labels and captions. Ask them to find the answer to the first question quickly and to raise a hand to show when they have done so.

- **Which has the longer legs – a frog or a toad? (AF2)**
- **What helped you to find the answer quickly? (AF4)**
- **How is a frog's skin different from a toad's skin? (AF2)**
- **If you were watching a moving frog or a toad from far away, how could you tell which it was? (AF2)**

Going deeper

- **Why isn't the text written in sentences? (AF4)**
- **What is the purpose of this chart? Who is it for? (AF6)**
- Do you think this is a good way of presenting information? Why? (AF6)

Reflect

Ask the children to suggest other pairs of similar-looking animals that could be compared using a chart like this: crane-fly and spider, male and female blackbird, fox and wolf, kangaroo and wallaby, duck and goose, cockerel and turkey, stoat and weasel. (AF4)

Task 6 Frogs and Toads

Spot the Difference!

	FROG	TOAD
Skin	smooth, yellowish brown, moist	dry, rough, bumpy, greyish brown
Head	narrow, pointed near mouth	short and broad, flat
Eyes	see all way round	see all way round
Tongue	long, very sticky tip	long, very sticky tip
Body	slim middle	fat middle
Legs	long at back, strong	shorter, fat, strong
Movement	hops, jumps, leaps	crawls, walks

TOAD

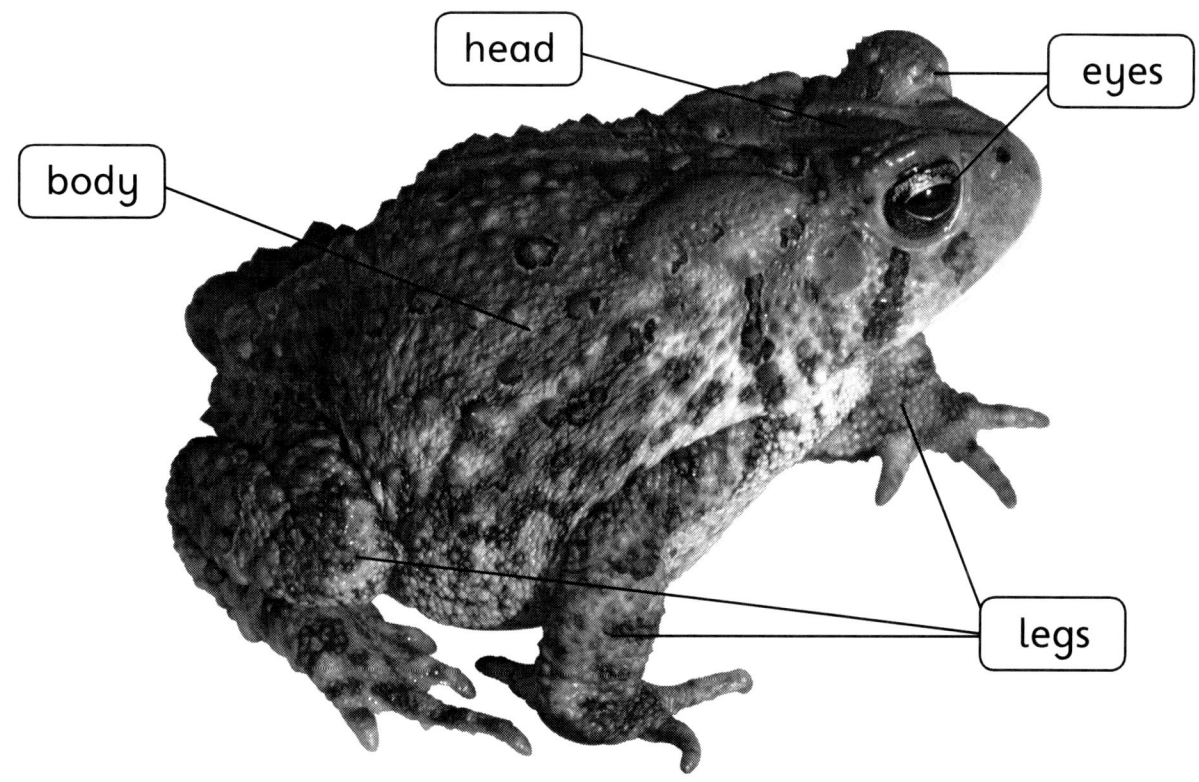

Task 6 Frogs and Toads

1. Which has the longer legs – a frog or a toad?

2. What helped you to find the answer quickly?

3. How is a frog's skin different from a toad's skin?

4. If you were watching a moving frog or a toad from far away, how could you tell which it was?

5. Why isn't the text written in sentences?

6a. What is the purpose of this chart?

6b. Who is it for?

© Pearson Education Ltd 2010. APP for Reading and Writing: Year 3

Task 6 Frogs and Toads

Main Assessment Focus: AF2 (understand, describe, select or retrieve information, events or ideas from texts and use quotation and reference to texts)

Question	Exemplified responses	Grid reference	Notes
Which has the longer legs – a frog or a toad?	Uses headings and pictures to find information.	Level 2 / bullet 2	
	Skims headings quickly to find information. Might quote the text.	Level 3 / bullet 2	
How is a frog's skin different from a toad's skin?	Uses headings and pictures to find information.	Level 2 / bullet 2	
	Skims headings quickly to find information. Might quote the text.	Level 3 / bullet 2	
If you were watching a moving frog or a toad from far away, how could you tell which it was?	Might read entire chart to find information to answer question – answer might include other factors as well as movement.	Level 2 / bullet 1	
	Uses headings to locate information on movement. Might comment that movement can be seen from far away but it's difficult to see details of skin, tongue and eyes from a distance.	Level 3 / bullet 2	

Main Assessment Focus: AF4 (identify and comment on the structure and organisation of texts, including grammatical and presentational features at text level)

Question	Exemplified responses	Grid reference	Notes
What helped you to find the answer quickly?	Might say he/she looked for where it says legs or looked at pictures.	Level 2	
	Points out or refers to headings and pictures/labels.	Level 3	
Why isn't the text written in sentences?	Identifies the table format and some features: 'It's a table. It has headings.'	Level 2	
	Identifies some basic features of the table: 'There isn't room, so it's in notes.'	Level 3	

Main Assessment Focus: AF6 (identify and comment on writers' purposes and viewpoints, and the overall effect of the text on the reader)

Question	Exemplified responses	Grid reference	Notes
What is the purpose of this chart? Who is it for?	Some idea of purpose and audience: 'People read it to find out about frogs and toads.'	Level 2 / bullet 1	
	Identifies audience and main purpose: 'To give children who are learning about frogs and toads information to compare them.'	Level 3 / bullet 1	

Exemplified responses matched to levels of attainment are provided as a guide. As always, professional judgement must be used when assessing pupils' learning progression and a range of evidence should be gathered for each AF.

Task 6 Frogs and Toads

1. Write three sentences about what a frog looks like.

   - ....
   - ....
   - ....

2. Write three questions to help someone to decide whether an animal is a frog or a toad.

   - ....
   - ....
   - ....

3. Make a 'Spot the difference table' for two other animals that are alike – such as a bee and a wasp or a tortoise and turtle.

Turtle   Tortoise   Bee

                                                  Wasp

Task 6 Frogs and Toads

A pupil response within the range for Level 2 might be:

Question 1 (AF6)
- At least two of the sentences are demarcated by full stops and capital letters. The sentences make sense and each one contains a verb.

Question 2 (AF6)
- Writes sentences that make sense as questions. Ends at least two of them with question marks. Main connective used is 'and'.

Question 3 (AF1, AF2, AF3, AF7)

AF1

Relevant ideas suggested: 'sting', 'colour', 'sound' etc.

Some repetition of ideas and information in body size and body shape.

AF2

Basic purpose established: presenting information about bees and wasps in a chart to help the reader to compare them.

Uses the main features of a chart: rows and columns with headings.

Some attempts to adopt the appropriate style: makes parts look like notes, but writes sentences rather than in note form.

AF3

Some basic sequencing of ideas: uses the headings on the chart to organise information logically.

AF7

Vocabulary is speech-like: 'how many times they want', but there are some adventurous choices of words: 'a darker shade than bees', 'hum and buzz'.

	Bees	Wasps
Sting	Bees can sting only once.	Wasps can sting how many times they want.
body Size	Bees are much bigger than wasps.	Wasps are much thiner than bees.
body Shape	bees are big and round.	Wasps are small and thin.
Where they live	bees live in a hive.	wasps live in a nest.
Colour	bees have black and yellow stripes.	wasps have a darker shade than bees.
Sound	bees hum and buzz.	wasps hum and buzz too.

Task 6 Frogs and Toads

A pupil response within the range for Level 3 might be:

Question 1 (AF6)

- Begins sentences with capital letters, ends with full stops. Uses commas if necessary, e.g. in a list of characteristics. Might use commas to separate adjectives describing the same noun.

Question 2 (AF6)

- Questions make sense. Accurate use of question marks. Some use of 'or' to connect phrases.

Question 3 (AF3, AF6, AF8)

AF1

Includes appropriate ideas and content: the appearance, movement, home and behaviour of the animals.

Elaborates on basic information using an adverb to modify an adjective 'slightly rounded'.

AF2

Purpose established: presenting information about dolphins and sharks in a chart with appropriate headings to help the reader to identify and compare them.

Awareness of the reader: humans might be interested in how the animals behave towards them and might need to know about their fins in order to identify them.

AF3

Attempts to organise related points: colour of eyes and skin.

Sequences ideas logically: behaviour – focuses on how the animals behave towards humans.

AF7

Simple, appropriate vocabulary with some descriptive words chosen for the effect of accuracy: 'squeaky', 'snappy', 'leaps', 'glides'.

Some limits in range: 'prey' might be more accurate then 'bait'.

	Dolphin	Shark
Eyes	Bright green	Dark brown
Colour	Greyish – Blue	Grey
Skin	Smooth, shiny	Smooth, damp
Behavior	Friendly towards humans.	Humans are bate.
Movement	Leaps, glides	Swims
Home	Deep underwater	Deep underwater
Fins	Thin, rough	Thicker, rough
Nose	Long, pointy, but slightly rounded	Long, pointy
Sound	Sqeaky	Snappy

Task 6 Frogs and Toads

Reading

Next steps for developing AF2

Children will benefit from further practice in understanding and retrieving information from the text. When reading a piece of non-fiction text together, ask:

- What is the information about?
- What similarities are there between [a frog] and [a toad]? What are the main differences? Where in the text did you find this out?
- What is the main idea in this paragraph / section?
- Where can you find information about...?

This activity should be part of a range of evidence gathered for AF2. Evidence for AF2 can be gathered from other sources, such as:

- observations during guided and shared reading;
- finding information from sources such as newspapers, leaflets, websites etc;
- research in other subject areas, e.g. finding information in geography, science, history.

All tasks in the book provide opportunities to gather evidence for AF2.

Next steps for developing AF4

Children will benefit from further practice in answering questions about the structure of information texts. Discussion points and questions like the following will help:

- What do you notice about how the text is set out?
- How does this help you to find out ...?
- How does the layout make it easier to compare [frogs] and [toads]?
- What different types of font can you find?
- Why does the writer use these?

This activity should be part of a range of evidence gathered for AF4. Other evidence for AF4 can come from sources, such as:

- discussions of other non-fiction texts, including reports and instructions;
- discussions of visuals from informative television programmes;
- guided and shared reading of online screen layouts.

Task 2 on pages 17 to 25, Task 3 on pages 26 to 36, Task 4 on pages 37 to 46 and Task 5 on pages 47 to 55 provide other opportunities to gather evidence for AF4.

Next steps for developing AF6

You could develop the children's ability to identify and comment on writers' purposes and intended audience though questions such as:

- What age group is the text written for?
- Why they might read it?
- Which words or phrases show the writer's interest or enthusiasm for the subject?
- How useful is the text?

This activity should be part of a range of evidence gathered for AF6. Evidence for AF6 can also be gathered from other sources, such as:

- observations during guided and shared reading of different genres of text, including narrative, non-fiction, plays and poetry;
- talking about radio and television documentaries and fiction;
- considering the intended audiences of various texts, broadcasts: how we can tell, and how they might be changed for a different audience;
- whenever a text is written for a specific purpose, including to instruct or entertain.

Task 1 on pages 6 to 15, Task 3 on pages 25 to 35 and Task 4 on pages 36 to 45 provide other opportunities to gather evidence for AF6.

Task 6 Frogs and Toads

Writing

Next steps for developing AF1

You could develop children's ability to make their information text writing interesting and thoughtful through discussion points and activities such as:

- 'Mind mapping': children write all they know about a subject, make links between ideas and then choose the most important information.
- Discussing information children have omitted and asking whether it is relevant: e.g. what an animal eats and what eats it.
- Making detailed notes when collecting information and then working with a partner to decide how much of it is useful.

This should be part of a range of writing activities from which evidence is gathered for AF1. Evidence for AF1 can also be gathered from:

- writing other types of information texts: e.g. a page from a guidebook;
- information writing in other subject areas such as history and geography.

Task 1 on pages 7 to 16, Task 2 on pages 17 to 25, Task 3 on pages 26 to 36 and Task 5 on pages 47 to 55 also provide opportunities to gather evidence for AF1.

Next steps for developing AF2

You could help the children to match their writing to reader and purpose by:

- Inviting peer-group feedback: what have they found out? How easy was it to find the information?
- Considering how to present information for a specific purpose: e.g. to help readers to compare two places, animals, plants, etc.
- Looking at devices such as numbering, using columns etc, and discussing which are useful in the text type they are writing.

This should be part of a range of writing activities from which evidence is gathered for AF2. Evidence for AF2 can also be gathered from:

- writing information texts for different audiences such as younger children;
- writing tables of information in different subjects: e.g. comparisons, fact files etc.

Task 2 on pages 17 to 25, Task 3 on pages 26 to 36 and Task 4 on pages 37 to 46 also provide opportunities for assessing AF2

Next steps for developing AF3

You could develop skills in organising and presenting information texts through discussion points and activities such as:

- What headings can you use to organise the information? Write a list and discuss with a partner and cross out any that do not fit in with the others.
- Discuss ways of recording information. Make a note of them: e.g. table, Venn diagram, graph, list, alphabetical order.

This should be part of a range of writing activities from which evidence is gathered for AF3. Evidence for AF3 can also be gathered from:

- children's recording of results of investigations or experiments in science;
- their written records of site visits or responses to questions in geography;
- non-chronological reports about historical topics: e.g. Viking settlements.

Task 2 on pages 17 to 25, Task 3 on pages 26 to 36, Task 4 on pages 37 to 46 and Task 5 on pages 47 to 55 provide other opportunities to gather evidence for AF3.